EVERYTHING®

C·R·A·F·T·S

BEAD
YOUR OWN JEWELRY

Step-by-step instructions for
creating one-of-a-kind
bracelets, earrings,
accessories, and more

Elizabeth Gourley & Ellen Talbott

Adams Media
Avon, Massachusetts

An Everything® Series Book.
Everything® and everything.com® are registered trademarks of F+W Publications, Inc.

Published by Adams Media, an F+W Publications Company
57 Littlefield Street, Avon, MA 02322 U.S.A.
www.adamsmedia.com

ISBN: 1-59337-142-X
Printed in the United States of America.

J I H G F E D C B A

Library of Congress Cataloging-in-Publication Data
Gourley, Elizabeth.
Everything crafts—bead your own jewelry / Elizabeth Gourley & Ellen Talbott.
p.   cm.
Everything series
ISBN 1-59337-142-X
1. Beadwork. 2. Jewelry making. I. Title: Bead your own jewelry.
II. Talbott, Ellen. III. Title. IV. Series.
TT860.G682255 2005
745.594'2—dc22
2004026844

Some material in this publication has been adapted and compiled
from the following previously published work: Gourley, Elizabeth &
Ellen Talbott, *Quick and Easy Beaded Jewelry* ©2002 (F+W Publications, Inc.)

Photography by Ellen Talbott.

This book is available at quantity discounts for bulk purchases.
For information, please call 1-800-872-5627.

Contents

. . . Contents

Welcome to the
Everything® Crafts Series!

If you want to get in touch with your inner creativity but aren't sure where to begin, you've already completed Step One—choosing the perfect resource to help you get started. The EVERYTHING® CRAFTS books are ideal for beginners because they provide illustrated, step-by-step instruction for creating fun—and unique—projects.

The EVERYTHING® CRAFTS books bring the craft world back to the basics, providing easy-to-follow direction on finding appropriate tools and materials to learn new craft techniques. These clear and readable books guide you every step of the way, from beginning until end, teaching you tips and tricks to get your craft to look just right.

So sit back and enjoy. This experience is all about introducing you to the world of crafts—and, most of all, learning EVERYTHING you can!

A note to our readers:
You're new to the beading world and you're not sure what it's all about, so you picked up this book to find out everything you need to know. There's plenty to learn! Read on to learn about the tools, materials, and techniques that will serve as a foundation for creating gorgeous jewelry perfect for you or your loved ones! There is something in *Everything® Crafts—Bead Your Own Jewelry* for everyone to create and be proud of.

This book would not be possible without the hard work of many, especially those at Krause Publications and at Adams Media.

—The Editors, **EVERYTHING® CRAFTS** *Series*

Introduction

Maybe you once visited a beading store and stared in awe at the wide assortment of beads—the variety of colors, shapes, and sizes. Perhaps you saw someone wearing a bracelet, necklace, earrings, or ring made with beads and thought, is this something I can make? Well look no further than *Everything® Crafts—Bead Your Own Jewelry* to guide you, the beginner, on how to create stylish jewelry pieces and accessories.

With many clear visuals and gorgeous projects, you'll learn the ins and outs of crafting jewelry worth giving to friends and family.

In the first section of the book, you will learn about the tools and materials to purchase for easy construction of jewelry and for building up your bead supply. The techniques explained here offer advice, tips, and tricks to set the foundation for your beading education.

So many people appreciate the value of something handmade. By spending some time learning and perfecting a craft such as beading, you'll never want to purchase jewelry that appears handmade again. And why would you? When you've become the resident beading artist, there's no stopping you!

Part One

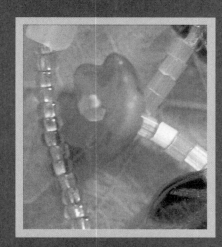

Beading Know-How

Tools, Materials, and Techniques

Tools and Materials

Tools and Materials

You can't get too far unless you have what's required for the projects that are found in the pages that follow. That's not to say that you should buy every type of bead mentioned here, or every tool and material defined and discussed. This is only a sampling of what most beaders might have close by. Don't worry, you'll start out with few beads, few tools, and few materials, and then you'll build your collection and supply of appropriate—and useful—tools. Read on to find out what will make your life easier.

Round-Nose Pliers

These pliers have tapering cylindrical ends perfect for making loops in wire or on head pins and eye pins. They can be used to hold small findings and are also useful for closing the loops on bead tips.

Chain-Nose Pliers

These versatile pliers have tapered half-round ends. They are good for gripping, crimping, wire wrapping, opening and closing jump rings, and squeezing bead tips closed.

Flat-Nosed Pliers

The flat-nose pliers have flat, straight ends that don't taper. The inside surface is smooth and won't make marks on the wire or findings.

Wire Cutters

There are two kinds of wire cutters. The side cutter and the end, or flush cutter. The side cutter has blades on the inside surfaces of the jaws and is good for cutting wire. The flush cutter has the blades on the tips of the jaws and is good for cutting things flush.

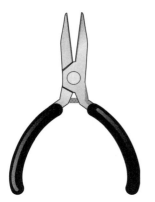

Round-Nose Pliers

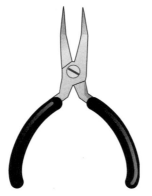

Chain-Nose Pliers

Flat-Nosed Pliers

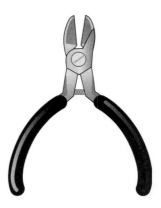

Wire Cutters

Scissors

Scissors are used to cut beading thread. We like to use embroidery scissors because their slender, sharp ends make it easier to cut the thread close to the bead. There is also a thread cutter that has no finger holes, has very sharp edges, and works well for snipping thread or cord.

Beading Needles

Beading needles have sharp ends and are shaped like sewing needles, but they are much thinner, have smaller eyes, and don't taper to the end. The eyes are small enough to fit through tiny bead holes. Beading needles come in several sizes based on their length and thickness. The lengths are approximately 1¼", 2", and 3". The 3" needles are used mostly for beadloom work. The most popular thickness of beading needles are from #10s (thick) to #15s (very thin). For the projects that follow, #11s and #12s were used. These sizes fit well in size 11° seed beads.

Twisted Wire Beading Needles

These needles are useful for larger thread or cord that won't fit through the eye of a beading needle. They are made of a length of wire twisted back on itself, so they don't have a sharp point. The eye is a large loop that collapses as it goes through the bead. Twisted needles come in four sizes: light, light-medium, medium-heavy, and heavy.

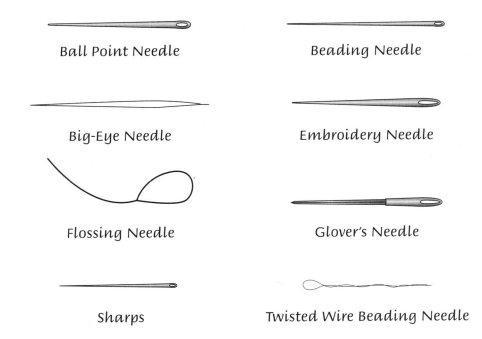

Ball Point Needle

Beading Needle

Big-Eye Needle

Embroidery Needle

Flossing Needle

Glover's Needle

Sharps

Twisted Wire Beading Needle

Jewelry Makers' Bead Boards

Bead boards are used to design and measure your bead strands before you string them. They are made of wood, plastic, or flocked plastic. They usually have inch markings along the strand indentions and have space for one to five strands, depending on the size of the board.

Beading trays work well to keep seed beads organized. You can keep the different color seed beads you might need for a project separated and the beads are spread out for ease in picking them up. Some come with lids for storage and travel.

Glue

Glue is an essential tool in making beaded jewelry. From securing knots to attaching beads to findings, you can find many bonding-cement type glues at craft or bead stores. The best glues will adhere to almost any surface and, when dry, will be clear, flexible, and waterproof.

Nylon Beading Thread or Nymo

Nymo looks like dental floss, and is great for using with seed beads and for making bead strands. It comes in black and in white as well as in a variety of other colors. The thinnest size is 000, medium-thin is size 0 or A, size B is medium, D is medium-thick and sizes E, F, FF, and FFF are thickest, respectively.

Silamide

This is a type of twisted nylon thread that comes in sizes A or 0. This thread is not as stiff as Nymo. It is good for seed beads or bead strands.

Kevlar

Kevlar is another seed bead thread that is very strong, since it is made from the same material as bulletproof vests. It comes in black or a yellowish off-white color.

Silk or Nylon Twisted Thread

This type of thread is used for knotting. It most often comes on cards, but you can get it on spools. The sizes on the cards are numbered, the thinnest being 0 and the thickest being 16. Some brands use the alphabet sizing with 00 for the thinnest, C and D being medium weight, and FFF being the thickest.

nymo

This is the most popular all-purpose beading thread currently available. Made of non-twisted bonded nylon filaments, Nymo comes in many colors and thicknesses. The number of filaments determines the thickness of the thread. Although Nymo has become the generic term for nylon beading thread, the brand name Nymo thread, by Belding Cortecelli, is generally the best quality. Nylon does not mildew or rot and makes a very durable thread for beadwork pieces.

Stretchy Cord

Stretchy cord is elastic cord used most often for bracelets and other jewelry. It comes in several diameters. Pick the one that fits through your beads the best. The thin size can fit through seed bead holes. The thinnest size is .5mm and the thickest is 2mm. They come in several colors, but the most popular ones are clear.

Stretchy Floss

There is also stretchy floss that looks similar to Nymo thread, but it is elastic. This type is harder to find and tends to fray, but is easier to knot than the stretchy cord.

Satin Cord

Satin cord is great for knotting or stringing a few large beads. It comes in many colors and three main volumes of thickness: 1, 1.5, or 2mm. Cotton or hemp cord is also made for bead use.

Leather or Imitation Leather Cord

Leather or imitation cord works great with large-holed beads. It comes in sizes from .5mm to 3mm.

Beading Wire or Tiger Tail

Beading wire is made of several thin wires twisted together and then covered with nylon. It comes in several sizes: .012 and .014 (thin), .018 and .019 (medium), .022 and .024 (medium-thick), and .026 (thick). Tiger tail is good for stranding and for beads with sharp edges that might cut through other beading threads. Crimp beads are used with tiger tail.

Memory Wire

Memory wire is a stiff, pre-coiled wire that will return to its original shape after being pulled apart. It is made in three coil sizes. It usually comes in packages with twelve loops of wire that must be cut to one loop for necklaces or from one to four for bracelets and rings. Memory wire is too stiff for jewelry pliers, so you have to use regular pliers when making loops on the ends.

Wire for Jewelry Making

Wire comes in gold or silver tone metal, aluminum, or precious metal. Wire known as niobium comes in many different colors. Beading wire is sized by gauges with 8 gauge being thickest and 34 being thinnest. Sizes 18-, 20-, 22-, 24-, 26-, and 28-gauge round wires are the most popular sizes for beadwork. Ultra thin size 34 is great for seed beads. Wire also comes in square, half-round, and triangle shapes. These are good for wrapping.

Spring Ring Clasp

Spring Ring Clasp

Clasps are used to hook necklace, bracelet, or anklet ends together. The spring ring clasps are circular in shape, and you need either a jump ring or a chain tab to complete the clasp.

Lobster Claw Clasp

Lobster Claw Clasp

These clasps are similar to spring rings in that they have a push tab to open them, and they close automatically when the push tab is released.

Hook

Hook and Eye Clasp

Hook and eye clasps are very basic clasps composed of a hook and a double ring end or a jump ring end.

Eye

Fold-Over Clasps

Fold-over clasps are the kind found on many watches or bracelets. The fold-over side goes into the bar side and folds over the bar and clips onto itself.

Insert-Style Clasps

These are usually fancy clasps that come in different shapes. Some are round, square, and some are the shapes of animals or hearts.

Barrel Clasp

Barrel or Torpedo Clasps

These look like little barrels when closed. They are screwed open and closed. Torpedo clasps are similar to barrel clasps, but they are thinner.

Torpedo Clasps

Tube or Slide Lock Clasps

These are clasps that have from two-to-five loops on one side of both ends to attach separate strands. To close the clasp, one side slides up and over the other side.

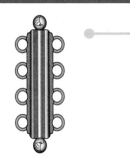

Magnetic Clasp

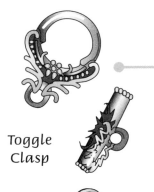

Toggle Clasp

Bead Tip

Jump Ring

Crimp Beads

Head Pin

Eye Pin

Magnetic Clasps

These clasps are simply two very small but powerful magnets set inside round clasps that have one smooth side and one side with a loop for connecting the jewelry strand. The two smooth sides are attracted to each other.

Fishhook Clasp

These are made with security in mind. One end of the clasp is shaped like a fishhook. The hook side is inserted into the other end of the clasp, over a little bar. Then the fishhook side is pushed until it snaps shut.

Toggle Clasps or Bar and Ring Clasps

This clasp consists of a large ring and a bar. The bar is longer than the diameter of the ring. Slip the bar into the ring by holding the bar in a vertical position. Then let go of the bar and it will go back to its horizontal position and be secure on the other side of the ring.

Bead Tips or Knot Covers

Bead tips are used to hide knots at the ends of necklaces and bracelets and have a loop at one end to attach the clasp to. There are three types of bead tips: standard, side-clamp-on, and bottom-clamp-on.

Jump Rings and Split Rings

Jump rings are rings of wire that are round or oval, soldered or non-soldered. They are sized from 2mm through 12mm and are sized by diameter. Split rings are rings of double wire and are used like jump rings. They range in size from 5mm to 28mm.

Crimp Beads

These are used instead of knots on beading wire. They secure the ends and help make the loop used to attach clasps. They are sized at either 2mm, 3mm, or 4mm. These beads can cut through thread or cord.

Head Pins and Eye Pins

These pins are very important in beaded jewelry making. They are used to make dangle earrings and bead links. Some head pins have flattened paddle-type heads instead of round beads.

Cord
Tip

Cone

Bead Cap

Cord Tips

Cord tips are used with cord larger than 2mm. There are two kinds of cord tip. The cord crimp has a loop for attaching the clasp and flaps that are folded over the cord end and squeezed tight. The second kind of cord tip is a cup with a loop on the end. The cord is glued into the cup.

Cord Coils

This kind of cord crimp is a length of coiled wire that has a loop on one end for attaching a clasp. It is slipped onto the end of the cord and then the coil farthest from the looped end is crimped tight.

Cones

A cone is used in multistrand jewelry to help hide the ends of all the strands. Cones have a wide mouth and a smaller hole on the other end.

Cord Caps

Cord caps are similar to cones; they look like cups with holes on the bottom. They are used for multiple strand jewelry to hide the knots.

Bead Caps

A bead cap is a little metal cup with a hole in the bottom which is strung on next to a bead so it fits over the bead like a cap. You can have one bead cap per bead or two, one on each end of the bead.

Bell Caps

These make any object that doesn't have a hole in it into a bead by giving it a hole without drilling. Use whatever size fits the object best.

Bullion or French Wire

Bullion is made from coils of thin wire, and is used to reinforce the section of beading cord or thread that is threaded through the clasp.

Bails or Triangles

These are used to make pendants. Some types are glued to the bead or stone. Others have prongs that fit into the hole of the pendant. Triangles are used when the hole of the pendant is too far down on the bead or the pendant is too thick to use a jump ring.

Spacer Bars

Spacer bars are used on multi-strand necklaces or bracelets. They are threaded on at intervals along the necklace or bracelet to keep the strands equidistant from one another.

Neck Wires

These are rigid rings of wire that fit around your neck. They come with a threaded-ball-screw clasp. You must use large-holed beads with these.

Ear Wires

Ear wires are meant for pierced ears. There are varieties of ear-wear for people who have pierced ears and for those who do not. Be sure to explore all ear-wear options to find items suitable for jewelry making for friends and family.

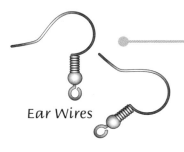

Ear Wires

Pin Backs

Pin backs are used for making pins or brooches. They come with flat, round, oval, or rectangle fronts where you can glue almost anything to make into a pin.

Barrette Backs

Barrette backs are similar to pin backs. They are found in longer lengths than pin backs and are used to hold hair up.

Fishhook
Ear Wires

Eyeglass Chains

These have loops on either end to hold eyeglasses. These can be made to suit anyone with glasses, based on color and technique selection.

Hoop Ear
Wire

Chains

Chains can come in bulk or can be sold separately. Two basic link styles are the cable chain and figaro chain. Chains can vary both in length and in weight.

Cable Chain

Figaro Chain

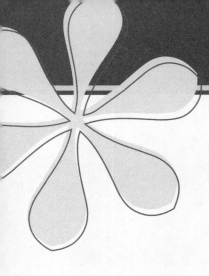

Beads

Anything with a hole through it can be considered a bead. Beads are made from many different things in many different shapes and sizes: metal beads, novelty beads, pressed glass beads, lampwork beads, pearl beads, semiprecious stone and gemstone beads, crystal beads, faceted glass beads, wood beads, horn beads, bone beads, shell beads,

bead finishes

It is also important to consider surface finishes and glass types when selecting seed beads. Some beads tend to visually recede (transparent, matte), while others stand out in the design (opaque, silver-lined, gilt-lined, iridescent, metallic).

Bugle Beads

Czech Seed Beads

Japanese Seed Beads

Faceted Beads

Tubular Beads

Pony Beads

Crystal Beads

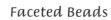

Delica Beads

Charlottes

and so on! A good rule of thumb is to purchase the best quality bead that you can afford. High quality beads will be more uniform in size, the holes will be larger and consistent in size and any surface finishes will be more durable. Check out the size and shape of beads you can find and use to create jewelry with, below.

Cloisonné Bead

Donut

Gemstone Chips

accent beads

Consider quality, color, and composition when selecting accent beads. Some patience and perseverance may also be necessary. Finding just the right accent bead is equivalent to finding just the right accessories for a new outfit. It takes time.

Hex-Cuts

Lampworked Beads

Liquid Silver Beads

Pressed Glass or
Molded Beads

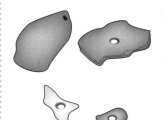

Shell Heishe Beads

Three-Cuts

Here are some charts to assist you in selecting the right size beads for your projects.

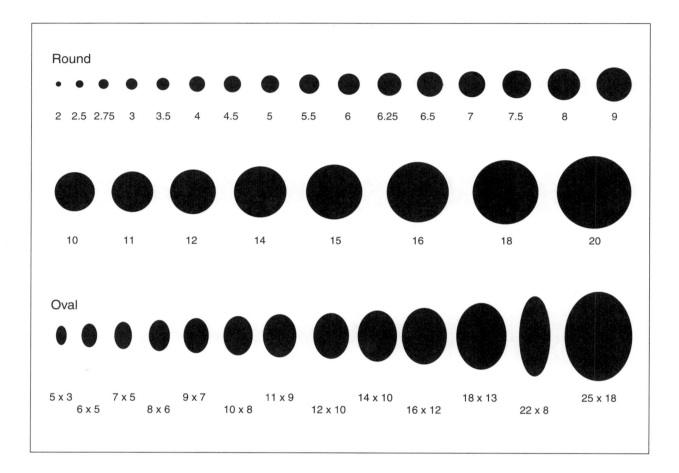

Round

2 2.5 2.75 3 3.5 4 4.5 5 5.5 6 6.25 6.5 7 7.5 8 9

10 11 12 14 15 16 18 20

Oval

5 x 3 7 x 5 9 x 7 11 x 9 14 x 10 18 x 13 25 x 18
6 x 5 8 x 6 10 x 8 12 x 10 16 x 12 22 x 8

bead trays

During the beadworking process, a "bead palette" will be essential. Some people make piles of beads on a piece of leather. Others use ceramic watercolor palettes. Still others recycle metal lids from jars, or plastic lids from potato chip, nut, or yogurt containers. Another option is a plastic six-compartment tray, with lids and pouring spouts, designed especially for beads. Whatever your preference, check the depth of the container. If it is too deep, it will be difficult to pluck beads from the tray.

BEAD SIZE	BEADS PER 16"
2mm	203
3mm	136
4mm	100
5mm	80
6mm	67
7mm	56
8mm	50
10mm	40
12mm	34
14mm	29
16mm	25
18mm	23
20mm	20

BEADING CHARTS

Here are the needle thicknesses that should be of help to you as you thread beads for your projects.

10 ━━━━━ ●	12 ━━━━ ●	14 ━━━ •	16 ━━━ ·	18 ━━━ ·
20 ━━━ ·	22 ━━━ ·	24 ━━━ ·	26 ━━━ ·	28 ━━━ ·

JEWELRY STANDARDS
Standard Jewelry Lengths (including clasp)

Bracelet 7" or 9"

Anklet 10"

Choker 14" or 16" depending on neck size; chokers fall just above the collarbone.

Princess 18"

Matinee 20"–24"

Opera 28"–32"

Rope 40"–45"

Dog Collar Snug-to-the-neck necklace of three or more strands.

Bib Necklace of three or more strands with each strand shorter than the one below it.

Lariat A necklace, 48" or longer, the ends of which are not joined; it is either tied or wrapped around the neck.

Graduated Necklace Necklace of any length with beads that gradually increase in size with the largest bead in the center and the smallest beads at the clasps.

Uniform Necklace Necklace of any length that has beads of a uniform size.

BEADS PER INCH ON A STRAND

Use this chart to figure out approximately how many beads you'll need for a project. All numbers are approximate.

seed beads

Size 16°	28 beads per inch
Size 11°	18 beads per inch
Size 8°	11.5 beads per inch
Size 5°	7.5 beads per inch

Seed beads are measured with degree symbol numbers. Size 24° is the smallest seed bead, size 11° is the most popular at about .09", and size 5° is the largest at about .22". Sizes 24° through 16° are very tiny and haven't been manufactured since the late 1800s. Most other beads are measured using millimeters.

round beads

2mm	13 beads per inch
4mm	7 beads per inch
8mm	3.35 beads per inch
10mm	2.5 beads per inch
12mm	2 beads per inch

Techniques

These techniques, shown here and on the following pages, are for a quick reference when you're in the middle of a project and you need a reminder on what to do next. They're here for you to practice basic methods of beading so that you can tackle any project in this book with ease.

How to Attach a Clasp Using Thread

Attaching a clasp using beading thread is quite simple.

1. Make sure to leave a fairly long tail on both ends of the piece. String one end of a clasp onto one end of the thread. Wrap the thread around the clasp loop several times, and pull tight. Tie a knot right below the clasp loop (**Figure 1**).
2. Repeat one or two times. Then hide the tail through a few beads. For extra security, tie another knot, if the bead holes are big enough to hide the knot (**Figure 2**).
3. Cut off the excess thread. Place a dab of glue on the first knot to secure it. Allow to dry. Using the tail of thread on the other end of the piece, repeat the instructions.

Figure 1

Figure 2

How to Attach a Clasp Using Crimp Beads and Tiger Tail

Attaching a clasp using crimp beads is one of the easiest ways to attach a clasp. Attach one end of the clasp before you start stringing your beads. Here's how to do it:

1. On the length of tiger tail or beading wire, string one crimp bead. Make sure that if you are using thin beading wire you use a smaller crimp bead and if you are using thicker wire or more than one strand of wire use the larger diameter crimp bead.

2. Slip the clasp loop onto the wire, then pass the wire back through the crimp bead, pulling tight so that there is just a small loop between the crimp bead and the clasp loop (**Figure 1**).

3. Crush the crimp bead, first with the crimping hole of the crimping pliers (**Figure 2**) and then finish it off by squeezing the dimpled crimp bead with the rounding hole of the pliers (**Figure 3**). When crimping, try to keep the wires separated so that one is caught on one side of the dimple and one on the other side.

4. Cut the excess wire about ½" from the crimp bead. String your beads making sure the first few beads go over both strands of wire to hide the excess tail. When you finish stringing on the beads, string on one crimp bead, and then the other end of the clasp. Pass the wire back through the crimp bead and pull tight, making sure the beads are tight against the crimp bead and clasp end. Then sequence the crimp bead with crimp pliers. Pass the tail end of the wire back through several beads then cut the excess.

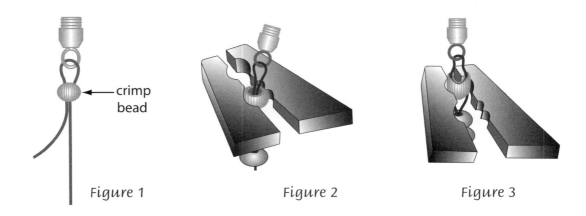

crimp bead

Figure 1   Figure 2   Figure 3

How to Tie Knots

The overhand knot is one of the most common knots. It is small, made with one thread (or many threads treated as one). Make a loop in the thread, bring one end of the thread through the loop, and pull tight (**Figure 1**).

1. The double-half hitch knot is used with a working thread and a stationary thread. Bring the working thread over and under the stationary thread, then under and over the stationary thread again and through the loop formed by the working thread. Pull tight (**Figure 2**).
2. The square knot is a very secure, widely used knot. It is used to tie two threads together. Bring the left-hand thread over and under the right-hand thread, then bring the right-hand thread over and under the left-hand thread. Pull tight (**Figure 3**).
3. To knot a bead strand, use overhand knots. To make the overhand knot as close to the beads as possible, put the loop of the knot on the middle of the bead, then hold the thread at the base of the bead with knotting tweezers, and pull the thread end tight with the other hand (**Figure 4**).
4. It is very important to tie the knots as uniformly as possible and to make all the knots go in the same direction. Do not over-tighten the knots, as this tends to make the strand bunch up or buckle.

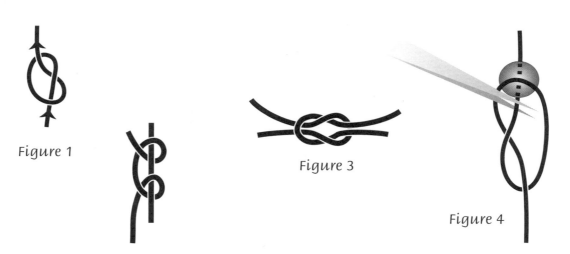

Figure 1

Figure 2

Figure 3

Figure 4

How to Tie a Stop Bead

A stop bead is used at the end and/or at the beginning of a strand of beads to keep the beads from falling off the thread, and to keep the tension of the beadwork tight. You can make a stop bead by tying a square knot around a bead or you can simply pass the needle through the bead twice. This way is not as secure as the square knot, but it is easier to remove (**Figure 1**).

Figure 1

How to Make a Jump Ring and How to Open and Close a Jump Ring

To make your own jump rings, get a nail or knitting needle with the desired diameter and wrap your wire around the nail or needle several times. Remove the coil from the nail or needle and, with side-style wire cutters, cut the coil down the center (**Figure 1A**). To properly open a jump ring, use pliers to spread the ends sideways away from each other (**Figure 1B**). Close a jump ring the same way.

Figure 1A   Figure 1B

How to Make the Square Stitch

Here is how to create this particular stitch method.

Row One

1. String on as many beads as needed for the project.

Row Two and All Other Rows

2. String two beads, then PNT (pass the needle through) (in the opposite direction of Row Two) the second-to-last bead from Row One and then back through the second bead just strung on (**Figure 1**).

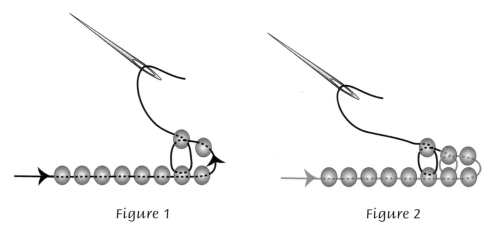

Figure 1   Figure 2

3. String one bead, then pass the needle through (in the opposite direction of Row Two) the third bead from Row One, and then back through the bead just strung on (**Figure 2**).
4. Continue in this manner stringing on one bead at a time until the end of a row. Remember to make a two-bead stitch at the beginning of each row.
5. To decrease at the beginning of the row, weave thread back through the previous row until the thread comes out of the bead where you want the row to start (**Figure 3**).

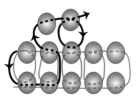

Figure 3

Square Stitch (continued)

6. To decrease at the end of the row, simply stop adding beads at the place you want the row to end.

7. To increase by one bead at the beginning of the row, string on two beads, PNBT (pass the needle back through) the last bead of the previous row. Then pass the needle back through the second bead just strung on (**Figure 4**).

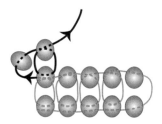

Figure 4

8. To increase by one at the end of the row on two consecutive rows, simply string on one bead and treat it as if it was square-stitched on that row. Then string on two more beads, then pass the needle back through the first of the three beads just strung on. Then go back through the first bead strung on, and then finish the row in the normal manner (**Figure 5**).

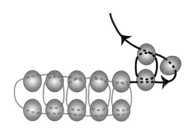

Figure 5

9. To increase at the beginning of the row, string on the desired number of beads, skip the last bead strung on and then pass the needle back through the other beads strung on. When you get to the body of the work, start the row as normal (**Figure 6**).

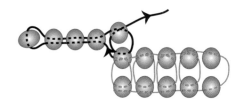

Figure 6

10. To increase at the end of the row simply string on the amount of beads that you want to increase by and, on the next row, treat them as if they had been square stitched (**Figure 7**).

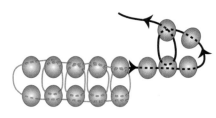

Figure 7

Part Two

Bead Your Own Projects

Jewelry, Accessories, and More

*I*t is customary to end memory wire with a loop; however, memory wire is very thick and it will bend most jewelers' round-nose pliers, so regular-strength round-nose pliers must be used. Here, a crimp bead and a bead tip were used to end the memory wire. You may use whichever technique you feel most comfortable with.

✳ Choker

Materials
1 loop of necklace memory wire, 14½" long
2 gold clamshell bead tips
2 crimp beads
48 gold-lined seed beads, size 11°
72 light iris transparent triangle beads
12 white star beads, 5mm
4 light iris transparent teardrop beads, 5mm x 9mm
6 gold AB bugle beads, ¼"
1 lantern-cut Swarovski crystal bead, 10mm
Flat-nose pliers
Crimp pliers
Flush style wire cutters

1 Slip a bead tip, then a crimp bead onto one end of the memory wire.

2 Crimp the crimp bead, using the crimp pliers, onto the very end of the memory wire.

3 Use wire cutters to trim off any excess wire sticking out of the crimp bead. Now slip the bead tip up to and over the crimp bead to hide it. Squeeze the bead tip closed over the crimp bead. Wiggle the hook end of the bead tip back and forth until it breaks off.

4 String beads onto the memory wire in this order: one gold seed bead, one triangle bead, one gold, one star bead, one gold, three triangles, one gold, one bugle bead, one gold, three triangles, one gold, one star, one gold, three triangles, one gold, one bugle, one gold, three triangles, one gold, one star, one gold, three triangles, one gold, one bugle, one gold, three triangles, one gold, one star, one gold, three triangles, one gold, one teardrop, one gold, two triangles, one gold, one star, one gold, three triangles, one gold, one teardrop, one gold, three triangles, one gold, one star, one gold, three triangles, one gold, one purple crystal.

5 Repeat this pattern backwards for the other side of the choker.

6 Finish the end with a crimp bead and a clamshell bead tip, repeating Step 1.

Continues

color and beads

The color you see in a bag or tube of beads is not always the same color that ends up in your beadwork. This is because of the many different types of glass used for beads and the finishes applied to them. Also, loose beads in a bag or tube show both the side of the bead and the hole. In most beadwork, only the side of the bead shows; hence if the bead hole has more color or a different color than the side of the bead, you will have a different shade of color in your beadwork than what appears in the bag or tube. Finally, beads of the same shade look different depending on whether they are made from transparent, opaque, satin, or another glass process. For these reasons, it is very important to make a test swatch of the colors you plan to use in projects with small areas of a variety or a gradation of colors.

✳ Ring

Materials
1 loop of ring memory wire, about 3⅝" long
2 gold clamshell bead tips
2 crimp beads
10 gold-lined seed beads, size 11°
15 light iris transparent triangle beads
4 white star beads
Crimp pliers
Flat-nose pliers

1 Attach a crimp bead and bead tip to one end of the ring memory wire the same way as described in Step 1 of the choker instructions.

2 String the beads onto the memory wire in this order: one gold seed bead, three triangle beads, one gold, one star, one gold, three triangles, one gold, one star, one gold, three triangles, one gold, one star, one gold, three triangles, one gold, one star, one gold, three triangles, one gold.

3 Attach a crimp bead and bead tip to the end of the wire.

seed beads

Because of their curved sides, seed beads are well suited for techniques where the beads are arranged diagonally or at right angles, such as knitting, crochet, right-angle wave, flat circular peyote, and netting. The curved shape of the bead fits smoothly together in these stitches.

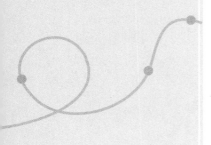

*W*ho says you can't make jewelry from lemons? It doesn't always have to be lemonade! These are fun to give to someone leaving for a sunny vacation on the beach or to a younger person.

❋ Necklace

Materials
Beading wire, size .012 to 1½ yards
2 gold crimp beads
34 yellow druk beads, 4mm
48 transparent yellow seed beads, size 8°
24 purple silver-lined triangle beads, size 6°
9 glass lemon beads
1 gold hook and eye clasp
Crimp pliers

1 Using about 1½ yards of beading wire, string a crimp bead, then one end of the clasp. Bring the wire back through the crimp bead. Pull tight. Squeeze the crimp bead with the crimp pliers. Cut the excess wire to about 1".

Attach one end of the clasp

2 String: one druk, one yellow transparent, one purple triangle, one yellow transparent, one druk, one yellow transparent, one purple triangle, one yellow transparent, one druk, one yellow transparent, one purple triangle, one yellow transparent. String on one druk, and one lemon bead. Make sure the first few beads go over both strands of wire to hide the excess. Repeat this sequence three times. Next string on one druk, one lemon, one druk, and one lemon. For the other half of the necklace repeat the sequence three times, then string on one druk, one transparent yellow, one triangle, one transparent yellow, one druk, one transparent yellow, one triangle, one transparent yellow, one druk, one transparent yellow, one triangle, one transparent yellow, one druk.

3 String on a crimp bead and then the other end of the clasp. Thread the wire back through the crimp bead and pull tight, making sure beads are tight up against the crimp bead and the clasp. Squeeze the crimp bead with the crimp pliers. Cut the excess wire to about 1" and hide the end by passing the wire back through the beads.

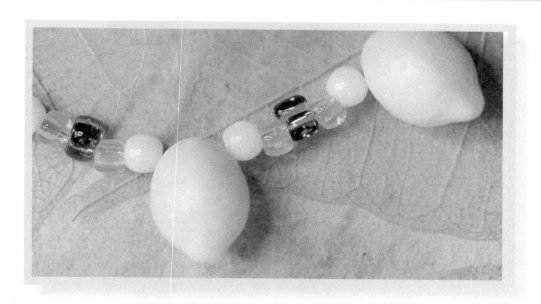

✳ Bracelet

Materials

1 yard beading wire, size .012
2 gold crimp beads
16 yellow druk beads, 4mm
16 transparent yellow seed beads, size 8°
8 purple silver-lined triangle beads, size 6°
7 yellow glass lemon beads
Crimp pliers
1 gold hook and eye clasp

1 Using 1 yard of beading wire, repeat Step 1 from the necklace instructions.

2 String one druk, one transparent yellow, one triangle, one transparent yellow, one druk, one lemon bead. Make sure the first few beads go over both strands of wire to hide the excess. Repeat the sequence six times. Then string on one druk, one transparent yellow, one triangle, one transparent yellow and one druk.

3 Repeat Step 3 from the necklace instructions.

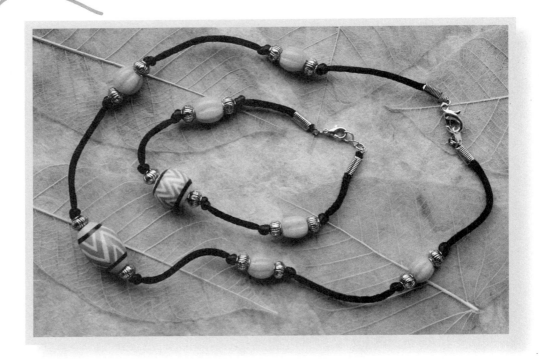

*T*he drape of a knotted necklace has a certain sophistication and grace. Knots add elegance to any necklace, but they also serve a purpose. Knots between precious beads, such as pearls, keep them apart so they won't rub against each other and get scratched.

✳ Choker

Materials

Black satin cord, 2mm, or 1mm if bead holes are smaller
10 metal accent beads
4 orange melon glass beads, 8mm x 10mm
1 oval painted wooden bead, 15mm x 23mm
2 crimp style cord tips, size to fit your cord
2 silver jump rings
Flat-nose or chain-nose pliers
1 silver lobster claw clasp, 15mm

1 Cut a 1-yard length of cord. Tie a knot about 4" from one end of the cord.

2 Pull snug. String one metal accent bead, one orange melon bead, and one metal accent bead. Tie another knot, making sure it is up tight against the beads. This is the first bead grouping.

overhand knot

An overhand knot is a good knot to use when weaving in threads. It catches the thread on itself, giving added protection against unraveling. To make an overhand knot, take a small stitch over a thread in the work and pull through until there is just a loop. Pass through the loop and pull tight. This knot is not as secure as the square knot but works well when used twice along with weaving the thread through several beads.

3 Start another overhand knot about 2" away from the last knot so that the cord between the knots will measure 1¾" after you make the knot.

4 String one metal, one orange, and one metal bead. Tie another knot. (All bead groupings will have approximately 1¾" of cord between the knots.)

5 The middle bead grouping is next. Use one metal, one oval wooden bead, and one metal bead. Now do two more orange bead groupings, for a total of five bead groupings; two orange groupings on both sides of the middle wooden bead grouping.

6 Cut the end of the cord 1¾" away from the knot on the end bead group. Slip cord tip onto the end of the cord. The end of the cord should be exactly even with the neck of the cord tip.

1 3/4"

7 Squeeze the cord tip around the cord with pliers, by folding one flap down flat and then folding the other flap on top of the first one. Then add the lobster claw clasp to the cord tip with a jump ring. Repeat for the other side of the choker. Finished choker measures 16" without the clasp.

 Continues

✳ Bracelet

Materials
Black satin cord, 2mm (or 1 mm if bead holes are smaller)
6 metal accent beads
2 orange melon glass beads, 8mm x 10mm
1 round painted wooden bead, 16mm
2 crimp style cord tips, size to fit cord
Flat-nose or chain-nose pliers
2 silver jump rings
1 silver lobster claw clasp, 10mm

1 The bracelet is made the same way as the choker, except it has only three bead groupings: one orange bead group, one round wooden bead group, and one orange bead group. There is a 1" length of cord between the bead groups.

2 Repeat Step 2 of the choker instructions, except have a 1" length of cord between the bead groups and the clasp ends. The finished bracelet measures 7½" without the clasp.

storage systems

Beginners often use something handy, such as cookie tins, to store their beads in. The moderately hooked will spend money on a storage system, i.e., a tackle box. The true addicts take over the spare bedroom and label it a studio and/or begin lobbying for an addition to the house.

*T*his collar project is actually for your pet! Believe me, when you put this on your dog to sport around town, everyone is guaranteed to take a second look!

✳ Collar

Materials
Nymo beading thread, blue (or color of your choice), size F
Beading needle, size 11
322 light blue druk beads, 4mm
16 light green druk beads, 4mm
8 pink druk beads, 4mm
1 blue olive shaped luster bead with a rose, 18mm x 13mm
1 blue round luster bead with a rose, 10mm
Scissors

1 Use about 3 yards of thread and leave a 12" tail. String on four light blue druk beads. Pass the needle back through the first three beads strung on. This forms the first stitch.

2 String on three more blue druk beads and pass the needle through the end bead of the first stitch and back through the first two beads strung on. This forms the second stitch.

31

Continues

3 Make eight more stitches using blue druk beads. Then make one stitch stringing on in this order: one green druk and two blue. For the next stitch, string on two blue and one green. Make six more all blue bead stitches, then one green, two blue, and then one more stitch of one green and two blue. Repeat this sequence two times, then make 10 all blue bead stitches.

Row 2

4 Pass the needle through the top bead of last stitch from Row 1. String on three blue beads. Pass the needle back through the top bead from Row 1 and then pass the needle back through the first of the three beads strung on. This is the first stitch of Row 2. String on two blue beads.

5 Pass the needle through the top bead of the next stitch from Row 1. Then pass the needle back through the end bead of the previous stitch and both beads just strung on. This is the second stitch of Row 2.

6 Then pass the needle through the top bead of the stitch from Row 1 and string on two blue beads. Pass the needle through the end bead of the previous stitch, next to the top bead from Row 1 and through the first bead strung on. This is the third stitch of Row 2.

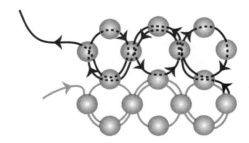

7 Make seven more all blue bead stitches. For the next stitch, string one pink bead and one green bead. Then for the next stitch, string one green bead and one blue bead. Next make six all blue bead stitches. Repeat the sequence three times then make four more all blue bead stitches.

Row 3

8 Using right angle weave stitch, make 46 all blue stitches.

9 Pass the thread through the end beads until the thread comes out of the end bead of the middle row. String on 12 blue beads and pass the needle back through the first bead of the 12, forming a loop.

10 Weave thread back through some of the stitches until secure and then cut off the excess thread.

11 Using the 12" tail of thread from the beginning of the first row, pass the needle through the end beads until the thread comes out of the end bead of the middle row.

12 String on two blue beads, one pink bead, the 10mm round glass luster bead with a rose, and one pink bead. Pass the needle back through the luster bead, one pink bead, and two blue beads. Weave thread through several stitches until secure and cut off the excess thread.

13 Using about 18" of thread, secure one end into the choker by weaving it through several stitches until it comes out of the twenty-third end bead, next to the middle of the choker. String on one pink, the 18mm x 13mm luster bead, and one pink. Pass the needle back through the luster bead and the first pink bead. Pass the needle through the twenty-fourth end bead next to the middle of the choker and then weave in thread until secure and cut off excess thread.

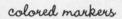

colored markers

Colored markers are useful for coloring obvious threads, or designs and patterns.

Continues

✳ Ring

Materials

Nymo beading thread, size F
Beading needle, size 11
28 light blue druk beads, 4mm

4 light green druk beads, 4mm
1 pink druk bead, 4mm
Scissors

1 Using about 1 yard of thread, make four all blue bead right-angle weave stitches. Make next stitch using one green, one pink, one green. Then for the next stitch, string one green, one blue, one green. Make four more all blue bead stitches.

2 String one blue bead; pass the needle through the end bead of the first stitch made. String one more blue bead, then pass the needle through the end bead of the last stitch made, forming a circle. Weave the end of the thread back through the stitches until secure. Cut off the excess.

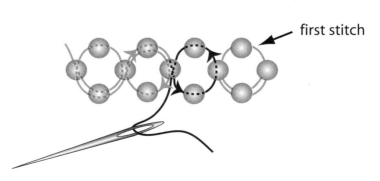

first stitch

Sparkly Silver and Black Necklace and Earrings

This sparkly duo goes well with that little black dress you've been dying to break out of the closet. Or, wear these on an interview for a touch of class.

Continues

Necklace

Materials

Beading wire or tiger tail, size .018
2 crimp beads
26 gray transparent silver-lined seed beads, size 10°
18 silver lined twist bugle beads, 15mm
4 metal accent beads
10 small silver flat flower or spacer beads
4 black oval faceted beads, 7mm x 5mm
2 silver bead caps
1 round faceted smoky gray crystal bead, 12mm
1 torpedo clasp (skinny barrel clasp), 10mm
Crimp pliers
Wire cutters

1 Cut a length of tiger tail 20" long. String on one crimp bead, and one end of the clasp. Then pass the tiger tail back through the crimp bead. This will form a loop with the clasp on it.

Attach the clasp

2 Pull tiger tail end tight so the crimp bead is close to the clasp. Leave a short 1" tail. Squeeze the crimp bead with the crimp pliers.

3 String on one gray seed bead, then create this bead sequence: one bugle bead, and one gray seed bead. Repeat the sequence, starting with the bugle bead, five times.

4 String on one metal accent bead, one gray seed bead, one bugle, one gray seed bead, one small spacer, one black oval faceted, one small spacer, one gray seed bead, one bugle, one gray seed bead, one small spacer, one black oval faceted, one small spacer, one gray seed bead, one bugle, one gray seed bead, one small spacer, one metal accent, one silver bead cap, one gray crystal (12mm), one silver bead cap, one metal accent, one small spacer, one gray seed bead, one bugle, one gray seed bead, one small spacer, one black oval faceted, one small spacer, one gray seed bead, one bugle, one gray seed bead, one small spacer, one black oval faceted, one small spacer, one gray seed bead, one bugle, one gray seed bead, one metal accent, one gray seed bead. Then string on one bugle, one gray seed bead. Repeat the sequence of one bugle, one gray seed bead, five times.

5 Attach the clasp end the same way as you did the other end. Leave a 1" tail and pass it through the beads until the tail is hidden.

silver linings

A silver lining in the hole of the bead gives a bright, shiny appearance and durable color to transparent-colored beads.

✳ Earrings

Materials

2 silver head pins
8 gray transparent silver-lined seed beads, size 10°
2 silver bead caps
1 round faceted smoky gray crystal bead, 12mm
2 silver-lined twist bugle beads, 15mm
2 metal accent beads
2 silver fishhook ear wires
Round-nose pliers
Flat-nose pliers

1 On a head pin, place one gray seed bead, one bead cap, one smoky gray crystal, one bead cap, one gray seed bead, one bugle, one gray seed bead, one metal accent, one gray seed bead.

2 With flat-nose pliers, bend the head pin close to the beads in a 90° angle. Slip on an earring wire, then with round-nose pliers make a loop, and cut off the excess wire. Repeat Steps 1 and 2 for the other earring.

Sassy Square Stitch Flower Brooch and Earrings

This project is quite simple to construct once you get the hang of the square stitch (pages 18–19). The earring flowers are glued to ear studs, and the brooch flower is glued to a pin back.

✳ Brooch and Earrings

Materials
Nymo beading thread, white, size B (or the size to fit bead holes)
Beading needle, size 12
210 pearly lavender seed beads, size 11°
2 yellow faceted glass beads, 3mm (for earrings)
1 yellow faceted glass bead, 4mm (for brooch)
3 gold seed beads, size 11°
9 green leaf-shaped beads
9 kelly green translucent seed beads, size 11°
90 white iridescent seed beads, size 11°
150 rosie lilac seed beads, size 11°
90 bluish-purple seed beads, size 11°
Scissors
Green felt
Bonding glue
1 small gold bar pin
1 pair of gold flat pad ear studs
1 pair of comfort clutch earring backs

1 Thread the needle on about 2 yards of thread. Using the square stitch and the design chart, make a petal. Increase on both ends of Rows 2 and 4, and decrease on both ends of Rows 5 and 6. Repeat four times for a total of five petals. Leave one yard-long thread end on one of the petals. Weave all the other thread ends into the petals. Each flower has five petals. This project needs three flowers so make ten more petals for the two earrings. Set aside.

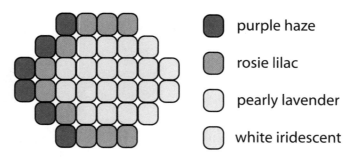

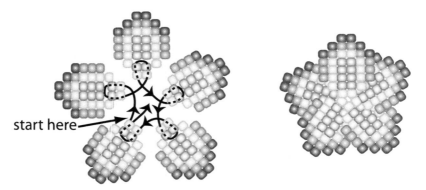

- purple haze
- rosie lilac
- pearly lavender
- white iridescent

2 Use 1 yard-long thread end to sew the petals together. Take five petals and sew them loosely together into a circle by passing the needle through the bottom lavender beads of each petal. It will be floppy, but that is okay. Arrange the petals so that they overlap and form them into a tight circle.

start here

3 Holding them carefully in order, sew the petals in place by passing the needle between the beads (not through the beads) and catch the threads. Keep sewing the petals, one on top of the other, until they are fairly secure.

4 Pass the needle up through a bead in the middle of the petals and string on one yellow faceted bead (4mm for the brooch and 3mm for the earrings) then string on one gold seed bead and pass the needle back through the yellow faceted bead and back down through the bead in the middle of the petals and out the back of the flower.

Continues

5 String on a leaf bead, one green seed bead, then pass the needle back through the leaf bead. Attach to the backside of one of the petals by passing the needle through one of the beads of the petal, making sure the leaf bead shows through two of the petals. It doesn't have to be too secure, because when you glue the flower to the felt the leaves will be held in place by the glue. Repeat two more times.

6 Cut a small circle of green felt about ⅝" diameter for the earrings and about 1" in diameter for the brooch. Put glue on the back of the flower and glue it to the felt circle. Make sure you arrange the petals and leaves the way you want them to look. Let dry. Then glue the flower and the felt to the bar pin back or the flat pad earring stud. Allow to dry. On these earrings you must use the earring backs with the large plastic circle around them, because the earrings are heavy and will droop if the backs are the small kind.

lap trays

Look for the type with a pillow attached to the tray. These are remarkably stable and make beadworking possible during long vehicle trips or while commuting.

*T*his necklace is composed of 53 beaded eye pins connected by jump rings. Wear this attractive necklace and matching bracelet with a dress that has an open neckline, and you'll be sure to dazzle your company!

✳ Necklace

Materials

53 gold eye pins
5 gold head pins
106 dark metallic with bronze finish seed beads, size 10°
53 matte metallic olive green seed beads, size 6°
5 black metallic finished faceted teardrop beads, 7mm x 5mm
42 gold jump rings, 5mm
1 gold lobster claw clasp
Flat-nose pliers
Round-nose pliers
Chain-nose pliers
Wire cutters

41

Continues

1 Slip one size 10° seed bead, one size 6° seed bead and one size 10° seed bead onto an eye pin. Using the flat-nose pliers, bend the straight wire above the beads at a 90° angle. Next make a loop as follows: With the round-nose pliers, hold the wire as close to the bend as possible and with your fingers or the chain-nose pliers, bend the wire around the top jaw of the pliers, pulling tight.

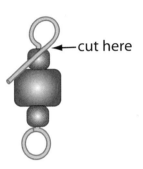

←cut here

2 Make sure the loop is the same size as the eyelet on the other side. Cut the excess wire and close the loop with round-nose pliers. (Determine where on the round-nose pliers it is the same diameter as the eyelet on the eye pin, and wrap the wire around the same spot every time you make a loop.) Make 53.

Main Chain

3 Open a jump ring, and slip the loops from two beaded eye pins onto the jump ring. Close the jump ring. Now open another jump ring and slip it onto the other loop of one of the attached beaded eye pins. Pick up another beaded eye pin and slip one of its loops onto this jump ring also. Close the jump ring.

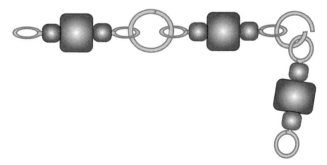

4 Continue adding a beaded eye pin to the chain until you have eleven attached beaded eye pins. To one end of the chain attach a jump ring and two beaded eye pins. Close the jump ring. Allow the first beaded eye pin to dangle and the other eye pin will be used for the main chain. Attach a jump ring with three beaded eye pins to the empty loop of the eye pin that isn't dangling (the main chain one). Close the jump ring. Allow the first two beaded eye pins to dangle and use the third one as the main chain. Attach a jump ring with three beaded eye pins to the empty loop of the main chain eye pin. Allow two beaded eye pins to dangle and use the third one as the main chain eye pin. Repeat this sequence four more times. Next add two beaded eye pins to a jump ring and the jump ring to the main chain eye pin. Allow one eye pin to dangle like the one at the beginning and use the other one as the main chain. To this main chain eye pin attach, with jump rings, 11 more beaded eye pins. The main chain is now finished.

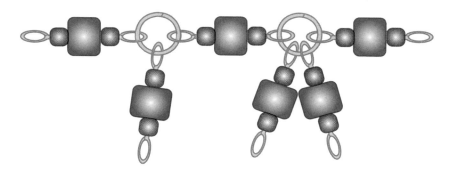

5 Put a teardrop bead onto a head pin and make a loop at the end as close to the top of the bead as possible. Make five and set aside.

Row 2

6 Open a jump ring and place one of the teardrop dangles onto it. Connect the first two dangling beaded eye pins on the main chain with the jump ring with the teardrop dangle on it. Close the jump ring. Open another jump ring and slip a beaded eye pin onto it. Connect the next two dangling beaded eye pins with this jump ring.

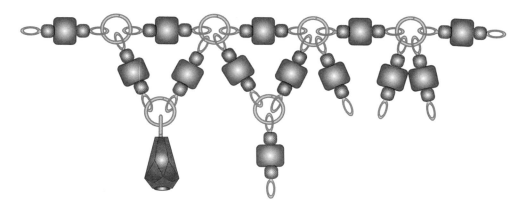

 Continues

7 Open another jump ring and slip two beaded eye pins onto it and then use this jump ring to connect the next two eye pins dangling from the main chain. Close the jump ring. Repeat this sequence twice.

8 Open another jump ring and slip on one beaded eye pin; use this jump ring to attach the next two beaded eye pins dangling from the main chain. Close the jump ring.

9 Open another jump ring and slip one of the teardrop dangles onto it and use this jump ring to connect the last two beaded eye pins dangling from the main chain. Close the jump ring.

Row 3

10 Open a jump ring and slip one of the teardrop dangles onto it, then use this jump ring to connect the first two dangling beaded eye pins from Row 2. Close the jump ring. Open another jump ring and slip on one beaded eye pin, and use this jump ring to connect the next two dangling beaded eye pins from Row 2. Close the jump ring. Repeat this sequence once. To connect the last two beaded eye pins dangling from Row 3, use a jump ring with a teardrop dangle on it.

Row 4

11 Open a jump ring and slip on the last teardrop dangle. Use this jump ring to connect the two dangling beaded eye pins from Row 3. Close the jump ring.

12 Attach the clasp ends to each end of the necklace using jump rings.

✳ Bracelet

Materials
28 metallic dark with bronze tinge seed beads, size 10°
14 matte metallic olive green seed beads, size 6°
14 gold eye pins
Flat-nose pliers
Round-nose pliers
Chain-nose pliers
15 gold jump rings, 5mm
5 black metallic luster finished faceted teardrop beads, 7mm x 5mm
5 gold head pins
1 gold lobster claw clasp
Wire cutters

1 Make 14 beaded eye pins the same way as in Step 1 of the necklace. Make five teardrop dangles the same way as in Step 3 of the necklace.

2 Using jump rings, make a chain with three beaded eye pins.

3 Put a teardrop dangle and a beaded eye pin onto a jump ring. Connect this jump ring to the three beaded eye pin chain. Let the teardrop dangle, then on the beaded eye pin attach another eye pin with a jump ring.

luster finish

A luster finish is a transparent colored coating. This is sometimes called a Ceylon or pearl finish if the coating is white, giving the bead a pearlized look. This type of finish has a good durability.

Step 2   Step 3

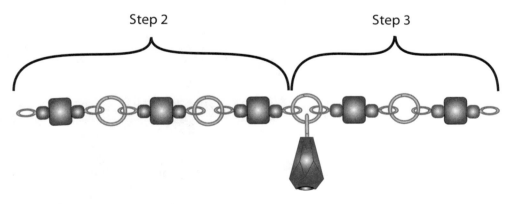

Repeat the sequence four times then add one more beaded eye pin.

45

Continues

4 Attach the clasp ends to each end of the bracelet using jump rings.

Wire comes in many colors, sizes, and metals. The sizes are determined by the gauge: The lower the number, the thicker the wire. Wire can be soft, hard, or somewhere in between. Soft wire is easily bent and hardens somewhat the more it is bent. Hard wire is more difficult to bend, so it is good for adding structure to a piece. Wires come in many shapes, including round, half round, square, triangle, and beaded. Square and triangle wire are often twisted to give added detail to a wirework piece.

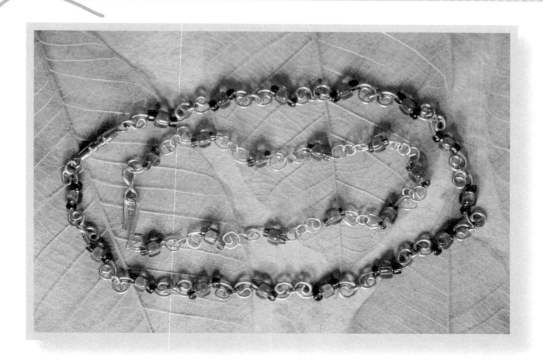

*T*here are so many different pieces of jewelry you can make by using this project. Use more beads for a stunning choker or necklace, or less for a stylish ring.

✳ Bracelet

Materials

26-gauge silver wire, about 18"
22 transparent green seed beads, size 10° seed beads
11 transparent pink triangle beads, size 6°
12 jump rings
1 silver hook-and-eye clasp
Round-nose pliers
Flat-nose pliers
Wire cutters

Continues

1 Cut a length of wire 1½" long. With round-nose pliers grab one end of the wire, placing the wire about ⅛" beyond the end of the pliers' nose and, using your other hand, wrap the wire around the jaw of the pliers forming a loop.

2 Release the pliers from the loop you just made and grab the wire just above the loop and wrap the wire around the jaw of the pliers, moving the pliers up the wire as needed to form a curve. Have the wire touch the loop after the curve has been formed.

3 Slip one green bead, one pink bead, and one green bead onto the wire end. Make another loop and curve on the straight end of the wire in the opposite direction of the first loop and curve.

4 Make 11 rosebuds (or enough to fit your wrist).

5 Using jump rings, attach the rosebuds together.

6 Use jump rings to attach the clasp to the ends of the bracelet.

✳ Anklet

Materials
20-gauge silver wire, about 24"
30 transparent green seed beads, size 10°
15 transparent pink triangle beads, size 6°
16 jump rings
1 silver barrel clasp
Round-nose pliers
Flat-nose pliers
Wire cutters

1 Make the rosebuds the same way as the rosebuds in the bracelet. Make 15 rosebuds (or enough to fit your ankle). You could also make more to make a choker or necklace.

2 Use jump rings to attach the rosebuds together.

3 Instructions for attaching the anklet clasp are the same as the bracelet instructions.

triangle beads

Triangle beads are triangle-shaped as you look at them through the hole. In beadwork, the side showing is either one of the flat sides of the triangle, or one of the triangle edges, giving a distinct texture to the beadwork.

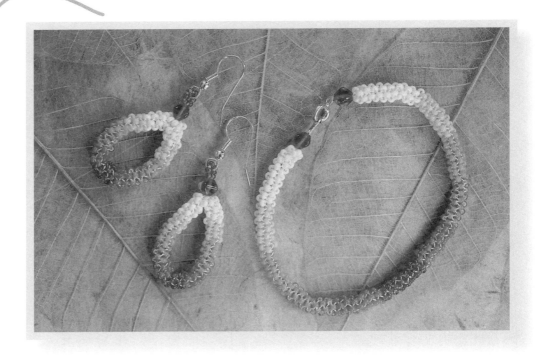

This jewelry set really does remind me of a sunset. The perfect complement to an outfit for an outdoor party, surprise your hostess tonight with a set created especially for her!

✳ Bracelet

Materials
Silamide beading thread, size A
Beading needle, size 12
5 gm yellow seed beads, size 11°
5 gm yellow-orange seed beads, size 11°
5 gm orange seed beads, size 11°
5 gm red-orange seed beads, size 11°
5 gm red seed beads, size 11°
5 gm dark red seed beads, size 11°
2 red accent beads
1 gold spring ring clasp

Rounds 1 and 2

1 Using about 3 yards of beading thread, string six yellow beads. Leave a 12" tail to use to attach the clasp later. Pass the needle back through the first yellow bead strung on forming a circle. These six beads will form Rounds 1 and 2.

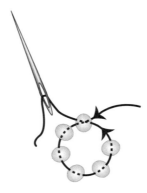

2 Keep the circle tight by holding the tail of thread. You will have three beads for each round. (This is called even-count tubular peyote because you start with an even number of beads, but the beads-per-round ends up being an odd number.)

Round 3

3 String one yellow bead, skip a bead from the bead circle, pass the needle through the next bead from the bead circle.

4 String one yellow bead, skip a bead, pass the needle through the next bead.

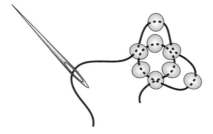

nail clippers

Nail clippers are ideal for trimming thread or soft flex wire close to the beadwork.

Continues

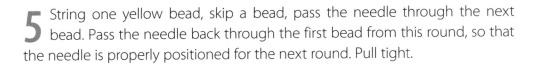

5 String one yellow bead, skip a bead, pass the needle through the next bead. Pass the needle back through the first bead from this round, so that the needle is properly positioned for the next round. Pull tight.

Round 4

6 After this round, it will be easy to identify which three beads are on each round. Three of the beads will definitely be higher than the three from the previous row. String one yellow bead. Pass the needle through the next stepped-up bead. Repeat this sequence two times. Then, pass the needle back through the first bead of the round so that the needle is positioned properly for the next round. Pull tight. Do ¾" of tubular peyote with the yellow beads, then change to yellow-orange beads for ½", orange for ½", red-orange for ½", red for ½", dark red for ½", red for ½", red-orange for ½", orange for ½", yellow-orange for ½", and yellow for ¾". (Note: 13 rounds equal about ½" and 17 rounds equal about ¾".)

7 When you are done with the last yellow round of the tubular peyote, string one red accent bead. Then string thread through the loop of the clasp. Pass the needle back through the red bead then through one of the yellow beads from the last row of the bracelet. Pull tight. Pass the needle back through the red bead, loop of clasp, back through the red bead then through the next yellow bead from the last row of the bracelet. Pull tight. Repeat several more times using a different yellow bead from the last row each time. Now pass the needle back through the peyote stitches until the thread is secure and cut off the excess thread. Repeat for the other end of the bracelet.

 ## Earrings

Materials
Silamide beading thread, size A
Beading needle, size 12
5 gm yellow seed beads, size 11°
5 gm yellow-orange seed beads, size 11°
5 gm orange seed beads, size 11°
5 gm red-orange seed beads, size 11°
5 gm red seed beads, size 11°
5 gm dark red seed beads, size 11°
2 red accent beads
1 pair gold fishhook ear wires

1 Repeat Step 1 of the bracelet except change colors as follows: seven rounds of yellow beads, five rounds yellow-orange, five rounds orange, five rounds red-orange, five rounds red, five rounds dark red, five rounds red, five rounds red-orange, five rounds orange, five rounds yellow-orange, seven rounds yellow.

2 String one red accent bead then string six dark red beads. Pass the needle through the ear wire loop then pass the needle back through the red accent bead and pull tight. Pass the needle through one of the yellow beads from the last row. Pass the needle back through the red accent bead and all six dark red beads holding on the ear wire. Pass the needle back through the red accent bead. Then pass the needle through the next yellow bead from the last row. Repeat one more time. Now weave thread through yellow beads until secure and cut off excess thread.

3 Thread the needle onto the tail on the other end of the tubular peyote. Pass the needle through the red accent bead, all six red beads, back through the red accent bead, through one yellow bead from Row 1. Pull tight. Repeat two more times then weave tail into yellow beads until secure and clip off any excess.

4 Repeat Steps 1 through 3 for the other earring.

*T*hese charming earrings and matching anklet will go well with whatever you wear. Casual and elegant at the same time, the metal gives just enough sparkle to catch one's eye.

✳ Anklet

Materials

Beading wire size .018
2 silver crimp beads, size 2mm (or size to fit your beading wire)
20 pink white-heart (or a color you prefer) seed beads, size 8°
5 silver metal flower beads, 7mm (or another kind of metal bead you prefer)
14 twisted silver metal bugle beads ⅜" long
1 silver spring ring clasp
Crimp pliers
Wire cutters

1 Using approximately 1 yard of beading wire, string one crimp bead, then one end of the clasp. Bring the wire back through the crimp bead. Pull tight. Squeeze crimp bead with crimp pliers. Cut off excess wire to about ½".

Attach one end of the clasp

2 String on beads in this order (make sure the first few beads go over both strands of wire): one pink, one flower, one pink, one bugle, one pink, one bugle. Repeat this five times then string on one pink, one flower, one pink.

String on beads

3 String on a crimp bead then a jump ring or tab (whichever you are using for your clasp), then thread wire back through the crimp bead and pull tight making sure beads are tight up against crimp bead and tab. Squeeze crimp bead with crimp pliers. Cut excess wire to ½" and pass back through the beads to hide.

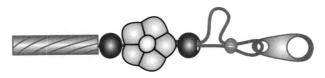

Attach the other end of the clasp

Continues

✳ Earrings

Materials
2 silver head pins
8 pink white-heart seed beads, size 8°
4 silver metal flower beads, 5mm
2 silver metal flower beads, 7mm
Flat-nose pliers
Round-nose pliers
1 pair silver fishhook ear wires

1 String beads onto head pin in this order: one pink, one small flower, one pink, one large flower, one pink, one small flower, one pink.

2 Using flat-nose pliers, make a 90° bend in the wire close to the last bead.

3 With round-nose pliers grab the wire as close to the bend as possible and, with your free hand, turn the wire around the jaw of the pliers into a loop.

4 Slip the earring wire onto the loop, cut the excess wire, and close the loop. Repeat these steps for the second earring.

wire cutters

Any wire cutter will do for beginning wirework, but as you become more adept, you will want better tools. The best wire cutters for jewelry close together parallel on one side, so you can make a clean cut through the wire, making a straight edge, rather than one tapered to a center ridge.

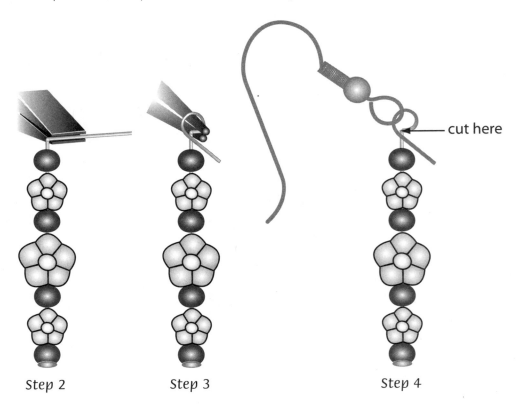

cut here

Step 2   Step 3   Step 4

This gorgeous jewelry set looks so good, your friends will wonder where you found such things. Try black or green beads for more beautiful-looking pieces you can wear when you go out on the town!

 Continues

❋ Necklace

Materials

18 gold eye pins (you might want to have a few extras), .021"

52 round faceted glass beads in various shades of red to orange, 3mm

34 round faceted glass beads in various shades of red to orange, 4mm

24 round faceted glass beads in various shades of red to orange, 5mm

1 smooth red glass teardrop bead, 13mm x 8mm

2 red faceted teardrop beads (with the hole running down through them), 7mm x 5mm

7 gold head pins, .025"

1 length of 24 gauge gold wire, 2"

2 gold jump rings

1 lobster claw clasp

Flat-nose pliers

Round-nose pliers

Wire cutters

1 Use darker beads for the middle of the necklace and then use lighter and lighter beads as you get toward the back of the necklace. Place one of each of the following, in the sequence given, onto an eye pin: 3mm bead, 4mm bead, 5mm bead, 4mm bead, 3mm bead.

2 Bend the end of the wire at a 90° angle using the flat-nose pliers as close to the beads as possible. With the round-nose pliers, grab the wire as close to the bend as possible and wrap the wire around the jaw of the pliers to form a loop the same size as the eye pin loop. (The round-nose pliers are tapered, so find a place on the pliers that is the same circumference as the eyelet on the eye pin and make the loops at this same spot every time—or you could use coil pliers.) Slide another eye pin into the loop you just made and cut the excess wire from the loop and close the loop with pliers.

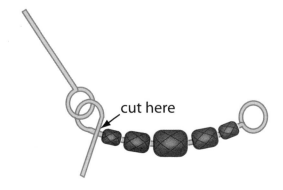

cut here

Page 106

Page 109

Page 22

Page 35

Page 41

Page 47

Page 89

Page 54

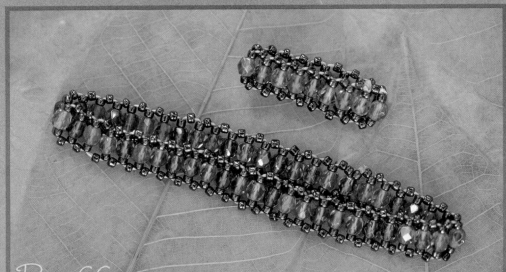
Page 66

Page 101

Page 69

Page 96

Page 73

Page 77

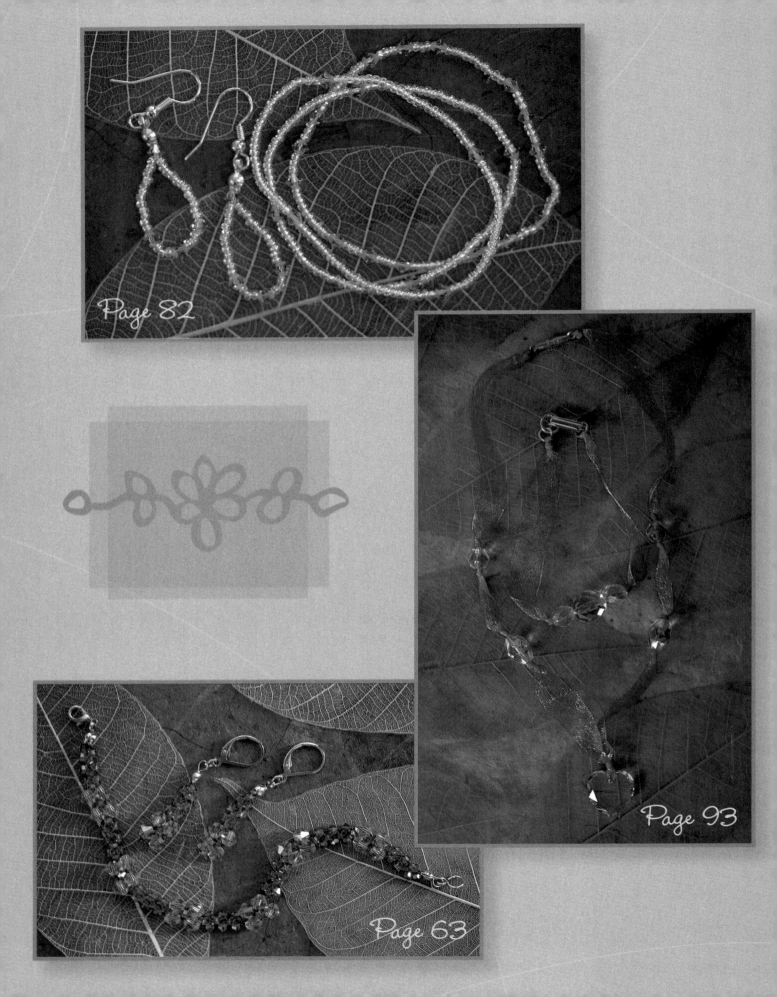

Page 82

Page 93

Page 63

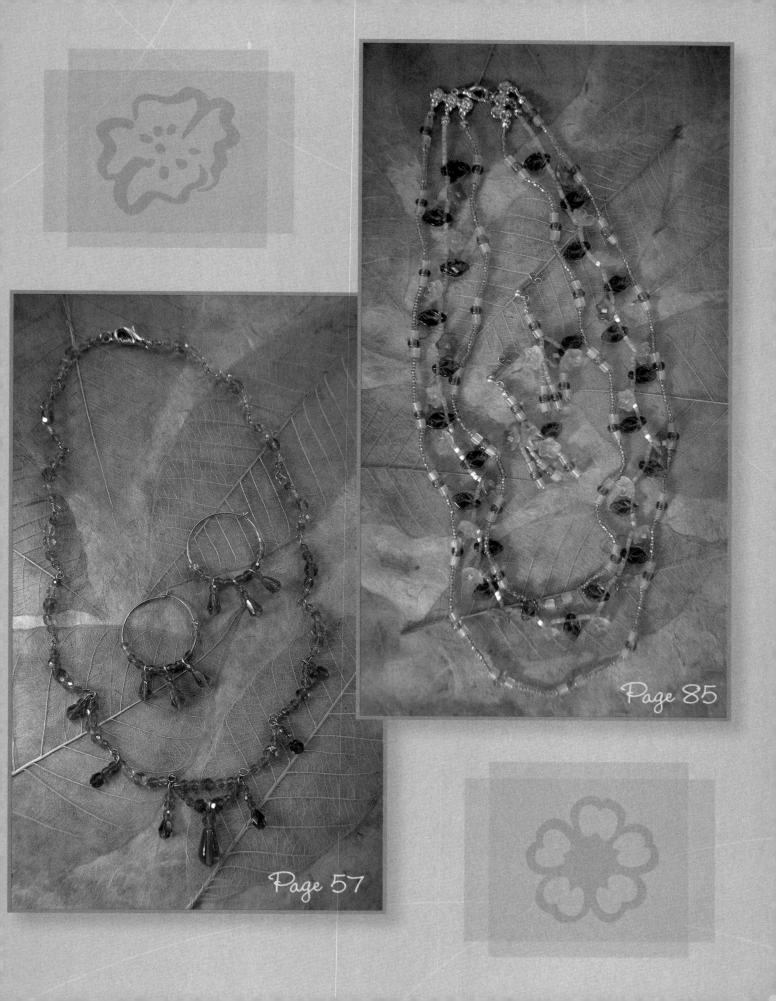

Page 85

Page 57

Page 28

Page 50

Page 25

Page 31

Page 38

3 Using your fingers, bend the eye pin with the beads on it into a crescent shape. Continue in this manner until you have eight beaded crescent shaped eye pins. Don't close the loop of the last crescent; set aside. Now make one more chain of eight beaded crescent shaped eye pins. Remember to leave the loop open on the last crescent.

4 To make the center dangle place the 13mm smooth teardrop, and one round 15mm bead onto a head pin and then form a loop and close it. Set aside and then make the two side dangles. Place a 7mm faceted teardrop bead and three round 3mm beads on a head pin, form a loop, but leave it open. Make one more. Set aside. There are four more dangles. Two with one 5mm bead and two 3mm beads on a head pin and two dangles with one 5mm bead and one 3mm bead on a head pin. Make the loops on these four, but don't close them. Set aside.

5 To make the center double crescent, attach an eye pin to the open eyelet end of one of the eight crescent chains. Also on this eye pin, attach one of the four bead faceted teardrop side dangles. Close the loops and make sure the dangle is attached under the crescent.

glass beads

Glass beads are made with a variety of finishes. Some finishes are durable, while others wear off easily. Finishes can fade in the sun, wear off from water, heat, abrasion, or oils in your skin. To test a bead for durability, let it sit in the sun for a week (in a clear bag in your car is a good place), sew a strand to some fabric and put it through the washer and dryer, or wear a strand of beads on your wrist for a week. If you find that the bead finish wears off, you may choose not to use it.

6 At the straight end of the eye pin attach a length of 24-gauge wire about 2" long by twisting the 24-gauge wire twice around the eye pin. Clip any excess wire.

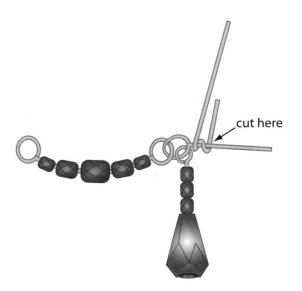

cut here

7 On the eye pin, place three 3mm beads, one 5mm bead, the center dangle with the smooth teardrop bead, one 5mm bead, and three 3mm beads. Form the beaded eye pin into a crescent, being careful not to let the beads slip off the end of the eye pin.

8 Take the 24-gauge wire and put on one 3mm bead, one 4mm bead, one 5mm bead, one 4mm bead, and one 3mm bead. Now wrap the end of the 24-gauge wire twice around the eye pin just above the beads. Cut the excess 24-gauge wire and in the eye pin make a loop right above the wrapped 24-gauge wire. Close the loop.

9 Slip the open loop of the other four bead faceted teardrop dangle into the eye pin loop just made, and then slip the open loop of the other eight crescent chain onto the eye pin loop just made and close the loops.

sensitive skin

Findings are metal parts used to put a piece of jewelry together. Try to use quality findings that will not discolor, break, or cause skin allergies for the wearer. Be sure to ask for hypoallergenic findings when you purchase them if you have sensitive skin.

60

10 Attach the three bead dangles on the crescents on either side of the center double crescent. Attach the two bead dangles on the crescents on either side of the three bead dangles.

place beaded head pins here

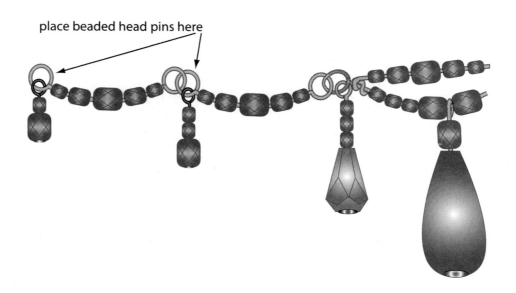

11 Put jump rings on each end of the necklace and attach the lobster claw clasp to the jump rings.

✳ Earrings

Materials

6 red faceted teardrop beads (with the hole running down through them), 7mm x 5mm
28 round faceted glass beads in various shades of red to orange, 3mm
6 gold head pins, .025"
Wire cutters
Round-nose pliers
Flat-nose pliers
2 gold hoop earring wires

Continues

1 Place one teardrop bead and one 3mm bead onto a head pin. Form a loop on the head pin as close to the beads as possible, cut excess wire, and close the loop with pliers. Make two. For the middle dangle, place one teardrop bead and two 3mm beads onto a head pin and form a loop, cut excess wire, and close the loop.

2 Onto one of the hoop earring wires string three 3mm beads, one two-bead dangle, two 3mm beads, one three-bead dangle, two 3mm beads, one two-bead dangle, and three 3mm beads. Bend the end of the hoop up at a 90° angle so it will fit into the hole on the other end of the hoop. Repeat for the other earring.

lighting

Adequate lighting is easily the most important consideration when considering workspace. Most desirable is a combination of natural and artificial light. Tired, strained eyes quickly turn beadwork into drudgery!

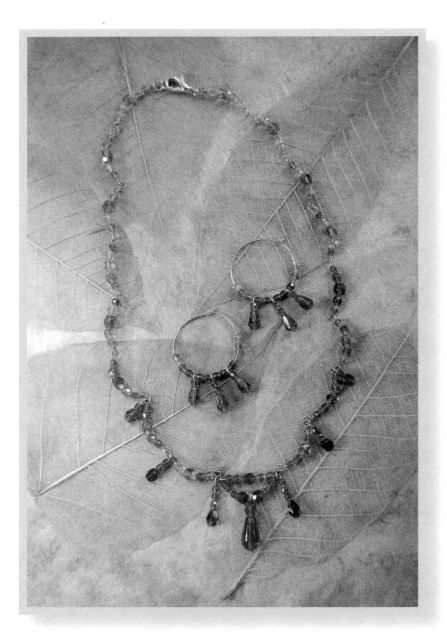

This dazzler speaks to a younger crowd since the colors are youthful, fun, and delicate.

✳ Bracelet

Materials

Nymo beading thread, black or purple, size F
Beading needle, size 12
75 purple Swarovski crystals, 3mm
24 pink Swarovski crystals, 6mm
2 silver clamshell bead tips
2 seed beads, size 11°
1 silver lobster claw clasp
Bonding glue
Flat-nose pliers
Round-nose pliers

63

Continues

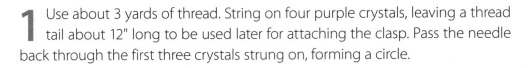

1 Use about 3 yards of thread. String on four purple crystals, leaving a thread tail about 12" long to be used later for attaching the clasp. Pass the needle back through the first three crystals strung on, forming a circle.

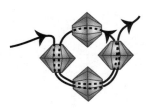

This circle forms the first purple "stitch." String three purple crystals and pass the needle back through the end crystal of the previous stitch and back through the first two crystals strung on.

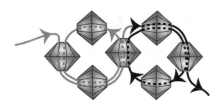

Repeat between the sequence one time, then string one pink, one purple, one pink. This forms the pink-purple stitch. Pass the needle back through the end bead of previous stitch and back through the first and second beads strung on.

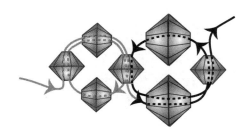

Repeat the sequence one time. This forms the "flower." Repeat the three purple stitches, two pink-purple stitches pattern five more times for a total of six "flowers." Add three more purple stitches to the end.

2 Thread the needle through the clamshell bead tip and string on one seed bead. Pull the bead tight into the bead tip and tie several knots around the seed bead. Place a drop of glue over the knots and bead, and squeeze the clamshell bead tip closed with pliers. Slip the clasp loop onto the bead tip hook and close the hook with round-nose pliers. Repeat Step 2 on the other end of the bracelet.

✳ Earrings

Materials

Beading thread of your choice, black or purple, size F
Beading needle, size 12
24 purple Swarovski crystals, 3mm
8 pink Swarovski crystals, 6mm
2 silver clamshell bead tips
2 seed beads, size 11°
Bonding glue
1 pair silver lever-back ear wires
Flat-nose pliers
Round-nose pliers

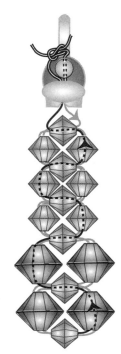

1 Use about 1 yard of thread leaving a 6" tail and make three purple stitches and two pink-purple stitches. Next pass the needle back through the stitches so that the thread is coming out of the same bead as the thread tail.

2 String both thread ends through a clamshell bead tip and one of the ends through a seed bead. Tie a square knot around the seed bead and pull tight, making sure that the knot and seed bead are snugly in the bead tip. Place a drop of glue on the knot and seed bead. Using flat-nose pliers, squeeze the clamshell shut. Slip the ear wire loop onto the bead tip hook and close with round-nose pliers. Repeat Steps 1 and 2 for the other earring.

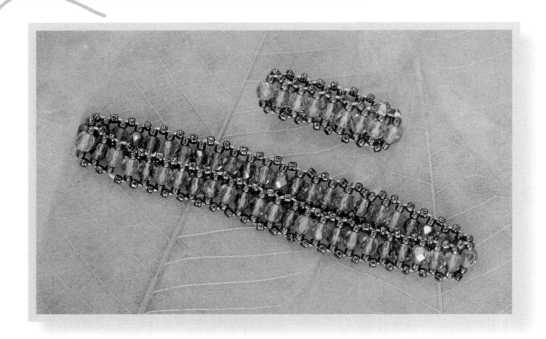

*T*here are many techniques for weaving beads into glass fabric that can be used to make stunning jewelry. Create this set for someone you love.

✳ Bracelet

Materials
Stretchy bead floss
2 twisted wire needles
Hematite Japanese seed beads, size 11° (or any metal color)
Faceted Czech fire polished beads in aqua, emerald, and peridot, 4mm

1 Thread a twisted wire needle onto each end of a six-foot length of stretchy bead floss. String on two seed beads, one Czech 4mm bead, and then two more seed beads. Position beads so that they are in the middle of the floss. Using the needle, string one seed bead, one Czech bead, and one seed bead.

2 Thread the right needle through the same three beads from Step 3 going in the opposite direction of the thread already through the beads.

3 Pull both threads tight until all beads fit snugly together. String one seed bead on the right needle and one seed bead on the left needle.

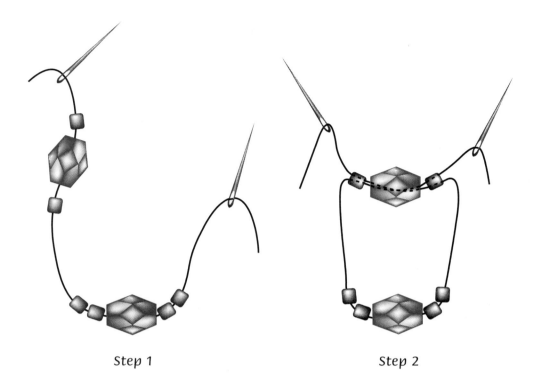

Step 1

Step 2

wire beading needles

Wire beading needles are a thin piece of wire, folded in half and twisted. The eye is the folded loop which collapses when pulled through a bead. Wire needles are used for threads which are too thick to thread in a standard beading needle, such as silk cord for knotted necklaces.

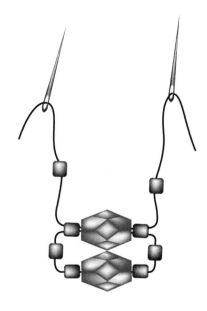

Step 3

Continues

4 Push beads down until they touch the other beads. Repeat the sequence until the bracelet measures 7" or the length to fit your wrist.

5 Bring the ends of the bracelet together and insert the needles (going in opposite directions) through the two seed beads and the one Czech 4mm bead on the end (the very first beads strung on). Pull both threads tight.

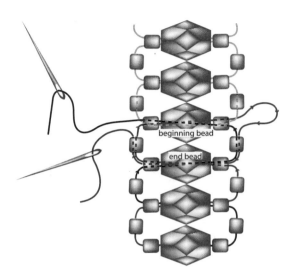

6 To tie the thread ends together, pass the right needle through two seed beads, one Czech 4mm bead, and two more seed beads, so that the two thread ends are right next to each other. Tie a knot. Secure the knot with glue, and slip thread ends into the beads next to the knot, making sure the glue goes into the holes also. Cut off any excess thread and let dry.

✳ Ring

Materials
Stretchy bead floss
2 twisted wire needles
Japanese seed bead, hematite or any metal color, size 11°
Czech faceted fire polished beads, aqua, emerald, and peridot, 4mm

1 Repeat Steps 1 and 2 from the bracelet, except make it 2¼" long (or the length to fit around your finger).

*H*eadbands made of fabric or manufactured with plastic are a thing of the past. Add some glitter to your appearance with dazzling beads! The matching necklace completes the look.

69

Continues

✳ Necklace

Materials
Beading wire, size .018, or sized to fit your beads
2 crimp beads, 4mm
White iridescent seed beads, size 8°
Light blue matte Japanese tubular beads
Green iris bugle beads, 4mm
White Japanese tubular beads
1 oval faceted glass light blue and green bead, 14mm x 10mm
1 toggle clasp
Crimp pliers
Masking tape

1 Cut three strands of beading wire, each 4 feet long. Slip a crimp bead on all three strands, then slip one end of the clasp onto all three strands. Pass all three strands back through crimp bead, forming a small loop. Squeeze crimp bead with crimp pliers.

2 String one of the strands with white size 8° beads, one with light blue tubular beads and the third one following this pattern: one white tubular, one green bugle, one white, one bugle. Make each strand about 10½" long. Tie a stop bead on each end. Don't worry about the beading wire getting a few bends in it since this part of the wire will be hidden in the large faceted bead.

3 Attach the end with the clasp to a table or to another flat surface using masking tape. Separate the strands and lay them flat. Braid them together: Take the strand on the right and bring it over the middle strand.

4 Next, take the strand on the left and bring it over the newly created middle strand.

5 Repeat until the braid measures 7½". When you get to the end you might have to remove some beads on one or two of the strands to even them up. All three should be the same length. Carefully remove stop beads, then hold the braid end tight in one hand, and string two white tubular beads onto all three strands. Push the white beads tight up against the braid, then string on the faceted glass bead and two more white tubular beads onto all strands.

matte finish

A matte finish is a dull finish achieved by tumbling or etching. This type of finish has a good durability.

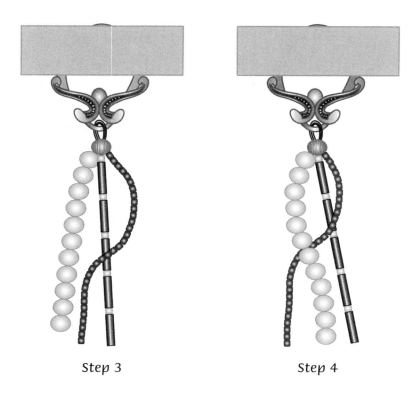

Step 3   Step 4

6 Remove the necklace from the table and string one of the strands with white size 8° seed beads, one with light blue tubular beads and one with this pattern: one green bugle, one white tubular, one bugle, one white. All strands should measure about 10½". Tie a stop bead to each end.

7 Braid the three strands together the same way you did in Step 3. When the braid measures 7½" stop braiding, and remove any excess beads and the stop beads.

8 String a crimp bead onto all three strands then string on the other end of the clasp. Pass the three strands back through the crimp bead and pull tight so that the crimp bead is close to the braid and the clasp loop is close to the crimp bead. Squeeze the crimp bead with crimp pliers and pass excess beading wire back through several beads then cut off the excess wire.

Continues

✳ Headband

Materials

1mm stretchy bead cord or size to fit your beads
Light blue matte Japanese tubular beads
White iridescent seed beads, size 8°
Green iris bugle beads, 4mm
White Japanese tubular beads
Bonding glue
1 large-holed green pony bead
Masking tape

1 Cut three lengths of stretchy cord, about 4 feet each. Tie a stop bead on the ends of each strand. String one of the strands with light blue tubular beads, one strand with white size 8° beads, and on the other one follow the pattern: one bugle bead, one white tubular bead, one bugle, one white. The strands should measure 32". Push beads tight together and then tie a stop bead at each end.

2 Remove the stop beads from one side of the strands, then tie the three strands together using an overhand knot. Attach the ends that are tied together to a table or some other flat surface using masking tape. Separate the strands and lay them flat. Braid them together: Take the strand on the right and bring it over the middle strand. Next, take the strand on the left and bring it over the newly created middle strand. Repeat until the braid measures about 21" or size to fit around your head. When you get to the end of the braid you may have to remove some beads on one or two of the strands to even them up. All three should be the same length. Carefully remove stop beads then tie the strands together using an overhand knot. Remove strands from the table.

3 String the large green pony bead on one end of the braid and push it over the overhand knot, then tie the two ends of the braid together using a square knot. Pull tight and cut off excess stretchy cord. Cover the knots with glue and slip the pony bead over the knots to hide them while the glue is still wet. Allow to dry.

This choker is made using a horizontal netting technique and is a perfect project for a rainy afternoon. Switch the colors to create a different look: soft colors for spring, dark colors for evening, and neutral tones for work.

✳ Choker

Materials

Nymo beading thread, white, size F
Beading needle, size 11
Embroidery scissors
40 transparent turquoise faceted glass beads, 6mm
39 milky white rondelles, 7mm
5 gms pearl white seed beads, size 10°
9 purple-lined turquoise faceted glass beads, 6mm
8 opaque lavender faceted glass beads, 7mm
2 light blue lantern-cut faceted glass beads, 5mm
4 capri blue lantern-cut faceted glass beads, 6mm
1 transparent turquoise faceted glass bead, 8mm
Bonding glue
Flat-nose pliers
Round-nose pliers
2 silver clamshell bead tips
1 silver toggle clasp

Continues

1 Use about 4 feet of thread and tie a stop bead to the end of the thread with a knot.

2 String on one transparent turquoise bead (6mm), one rondelle, one transparent turquoise bead (6mm), one rondelle, keeping this pattern for 14½". Tie on another stop bead as close to the beads as possible. Take the needle off the thread.

3 Thread a new, 2-yard length of thread onto the needle. Tie a stop bead. Pass the needle through the first 14 beads from Row 1. String on five white seed beads, one purple-lined turquoise bead, 5 white seed beads. Skip the next turquoise bead, rondelle, and one other turquoise bead from Row 1, then pass the needle through one rondelle, one turquoise, one rondelle from Row 1.

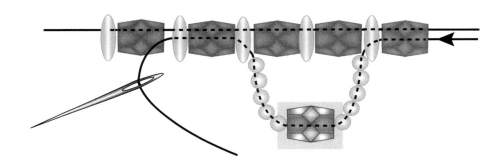

4 Repeat the sequence eight times. On the last repeat, instead of passing the needle through the one rondelle, one turquoise, one rondelle, pass the needle through the last 14 beads of the first row. Tie on a stop bead.

5 Using a new 4-foot length of thread, pass the needle through the first 14 beads from Row 1 and the five white seed beads and one purple-lined turquoise bead from Row 2. String on six white seed beads, one lavender bead, and six white seed beads. Pass the needle through the purple-lined turquoise bead from Row 2. Repeat this sequence seven times. On last repeat, pass the needle through the purple-lined bead and five white seed beads from Row 2 and the last 14 beads from Row 1.

6 Thread a new 4-foot length of thread. Tie a stop bead. Pass the needle through the first 14 beads from Row 1, through five white seed beads and one purple-lined bead from Row 2, and six white seed beads and one lavender bead from Row 3. String on six white seed beads, one light blue bead, six white seed beads. Pass the needle through one lavender bead from Row 3. Repeat the sequence two times except instead of one light blue bead, string on one capri blue bead each time.

7 String seven white seed beads, one turquoise bead (8mm), and seven white seed beads. Pass the needle through the lavender bead from Row 3. Finish the row to match the first half of the row with two capri blue beads and one light blue bead. Pass the needle through the lavender bead, six white seed beads from Row 3, one purple-lined bead and five white seed beads from Row 2, and the remaining 14 beads from Row 1. Tighten all strings.

8 Remove all stop beads from one side of the choker. Using all strands, string on a bead tip. Tie an overhand knot in the bead tip and while tightening the knot push the bead tip as close to the beads as possible. Cut off excess thread and place a drop of glue on the knot and squeeze the bead tip closed with the flat-nose pliers. Using round-nose pliers, close the bead tip hook over the loop on one end of the clasp. Repeat on the other side of the choker.

✳ Earrings

Materials
12 pearl white seed beads, size 10°
4 light blue lantern cut faceted glass beads, 5mm
8 milky white rondelles, 7mm
4 capri blue lantern cut faceted glass beads, 6mm
2 purple-lined turquoise faceted glass beads, 6mm
1 pair silver hoop ear wires
Flat-nose pliers

bead spills

Kids spill 'em, pets spill 'em, spouses spill 'em, even bead artists spill beads. A handheld vacuum is a good way to retrieve the beads quickly and easily.

Continues

lined beads

Lined beads are transparent glass with a color painted inside. They may fade in sunlight.

1 Onto one hoop earring wire, place three white seed beads, one light blue bead, one rondelle, one capri blue, one rondelle, one purple-lined bead, one rondelle, one capri blue, one rondelle, one light blue, three white seed beads. With pliers, bend up the end of the hoop so it will fit into the loop of the hoop.

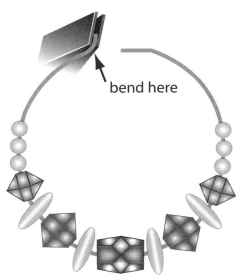

bend here

2 Repeat for other earring.

*C*reate this matching duo for that special someone who wears glasses, unless that happens to be you. Switch the colors of the beads for a look that suits you or your friend.

Continues

※ Necklace

Materials

Nymo beading thread, black or blue, size F
Beading needle, size 11
1 hank of crystal gold-lined seed beads, size 10°
187 matte silver-lined transparent teal size seed beads, size 6°
½ hank of opaque aqua seed beads, size 11°
2 large-holed turquoise beads, 10mm
2 silver eye pins
Bonding glue
2 silver cones
Round-nose pliers
Flat-nose pliers
2 silver jump rings
1 silver magnetic clasp

1 Use 1-yard lengths of doubled thread. Make four crystal gold lined bead strands, 17" long, one matte teal size 6° bead strand, 17" long, and two aqua size 11° bead strands, 17" long. Place a stop bead at each end of the strands and leave about a 10" tail at the ends.

2 Gather all the strands together and carefully remove the stop beads on one end of the strands. Tie all the strands together in a single knot. Make the knot as close to the beads as possible. Slip a large-holed turquoise bead over all the strand ends and the knot.

3 Tie the strand ends to the eyelet of an eye pin using several knots. Place a dab of glue over the knots and clip the excess thread ends.

4 Place one cone over the eye pin and make an eyelet on the end of the eye pin with the pliers. Attach a jump ring to the eyelet and one end of the clasp to the jump ring.

where did those beads come from?

Today, most beads are made in Japan, Czechoslovakia, or France. You can't always tell where the beads you have came from without verifying it with your place of purchase, but if it's on a hank, it's from the Czech Republic. It is the only country that does this right now; however, if it's in a bag or a tube, it may have been removed from a hank and bagged, so it could be from any manufacturer.

5 Gather the four strands of the crystal gold lined beads and twist together. Then take the remaining three strands and twist them around the crystal gold lined strands. Try to keep the aqua strands on opposite sides of the teal bead strand when twisting.

Twisting the strands

6 Carefully untie the stop beads from the ends of the strands, adjust the twists, if necessary, and make a knot with all the strands. Make the knot as close to the beads as possible. Slip thread ends through a large-holed turquoise bead and cover the knot with it.

7 Tie strands to an eyelet and attach a cone and the other end of the clasp as done in Step 2.

Continues

✳ Eyeglass Chain

Materials
Nymo beading thread, black or blue, size F
2 beading needles, size 11
168 opaque aqua seed beads, size 11°
28 matte silver-lined transparent teal seed beads, size 6°
378 crystal gold-lined seed beads, size 10°
2 silver jump rings
2 silver bead tips, clamshell style
Bonding glue
Flat-nose pliers
Round-nose pliers

1 Thread two needles each with doubled thread, about 1½ yards long. String a bead tip onto both needles and slip the bead tip down to the end of the threads and tie two knots in the bead tip. Cut off excess thread and place a drop of glue on the knots. Squeeze the bead tip closed over the knots with the flat-nose pliers. Next, using both needles, string on three aqua beads, one teal bead, three aqua.

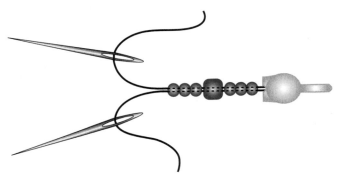

2 String seven crystal gold-lined beads onto one needle, then do the same for the other needle.

3 Repeat between the sequence 26 more times, and to finish it off string three aqua, one teal, and three aqua. The piece should measure 25".

4 Attach a bead tip the same way as in Step 1, making sure you keep the bead tip close to the end beads. Slip the eyeglass chain finding onto the hook of the bead tip and turn the hook closed with the round-nose pliers. Do the same for the other end.

sewing standby

Fray Check is an old sewing standby. It is useful for stiffening the end of the thread for easier threading into the eye of the needle. A light coating of glue will also work to create a stiff thread end that can function like a self-needle.

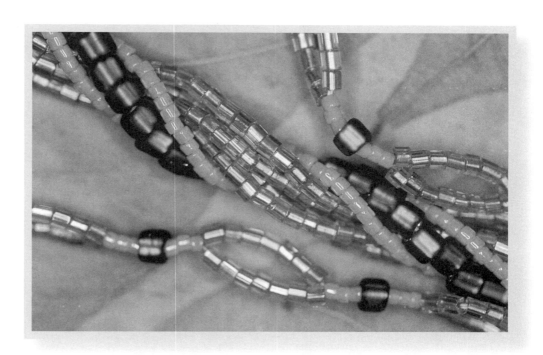

A closeup of the finished project

These bouncy bracelets and matching earrings are perfect for energetic kids or anyone who wants to feel like one. Just working with the stretchy floss in making them will make you giddy.

✳ Bracelet

Materials
White stretchy floss (fibrous elastic) or .5mm clear stretchy cord
Twisted wire bead needle
23 lantern-cut Swarovski crystals, 4mm
1 small tube of light pink seed beads, size 11°
Bonding glue

1 Using about 1 yard of floss and the twisted beading needle, string 31 light pink beads, then one crystal. Repeat three times. Strand should measure 7". Make one more. Then for the third bracelet, string beads in the following pattern: 10 light pink, one crystal, three pink, one crystal, three pink, one crystal. Repeat four times.

2 When you are done stringing the beads, tie a square knot (right over left, then left over right), keeping the beads tightly together. Thread the tails into the beads on either side of the knot. Place a dab of glue on the knot and wiggle it so the glue also goes into the holes of the beads on either side to hold the tails in the beads. Let dry, then cut off excess floss. Repeat for each bracelet.

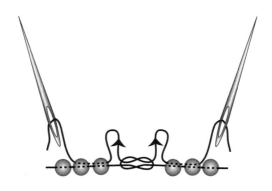

delicate finishes

Beads with delicate finishes are sometimes the most beautiful or the perfect ones for your project. That's when you have to decide how much handling your piece will have, and whether it will hold up over time. Sometimes it's better to change bead colors to make a lasting project, but other times you may just want to use the beads you've found.

✳ ## Earrings

Materials
Beading needle, size 12
White beading thread
8 lantern cut Swarovski crystals, 4mm
62 light pink seed beads, size 11°
2 bead tips
2 lever back ear wires
Flat-nose pliers
Round-nose pliers
Bonding glue

1 Thread a beading needle with about 1 yard of beading thread.

Continues

2 String on one clamshell bead tip, one crystal, 12 pink seed beads, one crystal, three pink, one crystal, three pink, one crystal, 12 pink. Pass the needle back through the first crystal and bead tip forming a loop.

3 String on one pink seed bead and tie a square knot using both thread ends.

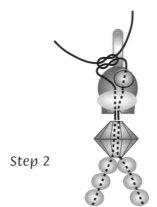

Step 2

Step 3

4 Place a drop of glue on the knot and squeeze the bead tip closed (using flat-nose pliers) over the knot and the seed bead.

5 Slip the earring wire onto the bead tip and using the round-nose pliers turn the bead tip hook closed around the earring wire loop. Repeat Steps 1 and 2 for the second earring.

*W*hen completed, this necklace and earring set will look just like you plucked it out of a garden. The myriad of colors and textures that blend together help to give the beads in this piece a truly organic look.

Continues

Necklace

Materials

Nymo beading thread, light brown or tan, size F
Beading needle, size 11
23 transparent green leaf beads
8 dark pink flower beads with the hole in the middle
7 light amber flower beads
7 light pink flower beads
10 gms bronze silver-lined seed beads, size 11°
34 transparent amber seed beads, size 8°
68 matte light amber square beads, 3.5mm x 4mm
196 light yellow satin beads
1 gold lobster claw clasp
2 jump rings
2 three-strand separators
6 gold bead tips
Round-nose pliers
Flat-nose pliers
Scissors

1 Thread a needle with doubled thread 2 yards long. Attach a bead tip to the end of the thread. * String on one square bead, one size 8° amber bead, one square bead, 15 bronze size 11° seed beads. * Repeat between asterisks 17 times then string on one square bead, one size 8° amber bead, one square bead. Attach bead tip to the end and set aside. The strand should measure 22½" (excluding the bead tips).

2 Thread the needle with doubled thread 2 yards long. Attach a bead tip to the end of the thread. String on 10 satin beads, one leaf bead, * four satin beads, one dark pink flower bead, one satin bead, and then pass the needle back through the flower bead. When stringing on the flower bead, PNT the backside of the flower first and then BT the front of the bead.

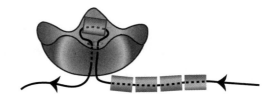

3 String on four satin beads, one leaf bead, four satin beads, one light pink flower bead, one satin bead, pass the needle back through the flower bead. String on four satin beads, one leaf bead, four satin beads, one light amber flower bead, one satin bead, pass the needle back through the flower bead. String on four satin beads, one leaf bead. * Repeat between asterisks six times then string on four satin beads, one dark pink flower bead, one satin bead, PNBT flower bead. String on four satin beads, one leaf bead, 10 satin beads. Attach a bead tip as close to the beads as possible. Strand should measure 20¼" excluding bead tips. When stringing this strand make sure you push the flower beads close to their neighboring beads, so that you won't get unsightly gaps in the bead strand.

4 Thread a needle with about 2 yards of doubled thread. Attach a bead tip at the end of the thread. String 10 bronze size 11° seed beads, * one square bead, one amber size 8° bead, one square bead, 15 bronze size 11° beads. * Repeat between the asterisks 13 times then string on one square bead, one amber size 8° bead, one square bead, and 10 bronze size 11° seed beads. Attach a bead tip as close to the beads as possible. The strand should measure 18½" excluding the bead tip.

5 Hold the two separators with the one-loop-edge on top and the three-loop-edge on the bottom, then attach Strand #1 to the right-most loop on the right-hand-side separator and the left-most loop on the left-hand-side separator, so Strand #1 becomes the bottom-most strand. Attach Strand #2 to the middle loops and it becomes the middle strand. Attach Strand #3 to the remaining loops and it becomes the top strand. Now attach the clasp ends to the separators.

Continues

✳ Earrings

Materials

Nymo beading thread, light brown or tan, size F
Beading needle, size 11
2 transparent green leaf beads
2 dark pink flower beads with the hole in the middle
2 light amber flower beads
2 light pink flower beads
6 bronze silver lined seed beads, size 11°
8 transparent amber seed beads, size 8°
16 matte light amber square beads, 3.5mm x 4mm
56 light yellow satin beads
1 pair gold drop ear studs
2 gold bead tips
Round-nose pliers
Flat-nose pliers
Scissors

Step 1

1 Thread needle with about 1 yard of thread and string on one square bead, one amber size 8° bead, one square bead, four satins. String on one dark pink flower bead, one satin bead and PNBT flower bead. (See Step 1 art from the necklace.) String on six satins, one square, one amber size 8°, one square, and one bronze seed bead. PNBT one square, one size 8°, one square, six satins, four satins.

2 For the next dangle, string on four satin, one leaf, one light amber flower, one satin, PNBT the flower bead. String on four satins, four squares, one size 8°, one square, one bronze. PNBT one square, one size 8°, one square, four satins, one leaf, four satins. For third dangle, string on four satins, one light pink flower, one satin, PNBT flower bead. String on six satins, one square, one size 8°, one square, one bronze. PNBT one square, one size 8°, one square, six satins, four satins, and then PNBT the first square, one size 8° and one square bead strung on. String on bead tip with both thread ends and attach bead tip to thread and then attach drop ear stud to bead tip. Make two.

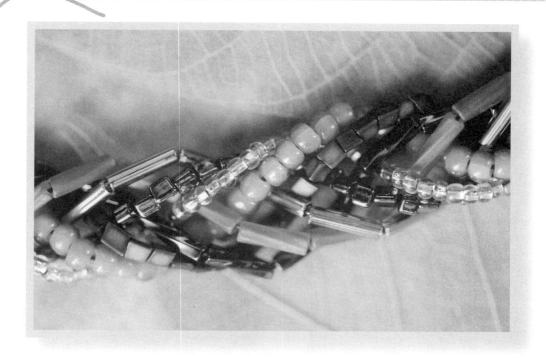

$\mathscr{I}$f seven is your lucky number, than this charming set is for you. But considering how stunning you'll look with both your hair and wrist artfully decorated, you won't need a lot of luck to attract attention.

✳ Bracelet

Materials

Nymo beading thread, black, size B

Beading needle, size 12, or whatever size fits your beads

Gold lined seed beads, size 11°

Pink white heart seed beads, size 8°

Blue iris twist bugle beads, ¼" long

Gold AB luster bugle beads, ¼" long

Pink matte twist bugle beads, ¼" long

Bronze triangle beads

Matte iris AB triangle beads

2 gold cones

2 gold clamshells

1 gold lobster claw clasp

2 gold jump rings

Bonding glue

Masking tape

Continues

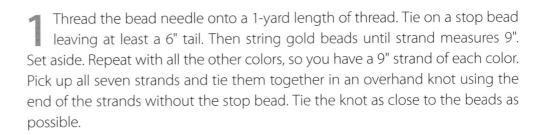

1 Thread the bead needle onto a 1-yard length of thread. Tie on a stop bead leaving at least a 6" tail. Then string gold beads until strand measures 9". Set aside. Repeat with all the other colors, so you have a 9" strand of each color. Pick up all seven strands and tie them together in an overhand knot using the end of the strands without the stop bead. Tie the knot as close to the beads as possible.

2 Attach the knot to a table or other flat surface using masking tape. Lay all the strands flat. * Pick up the right-most strand and bring it over three strands then lay it down.

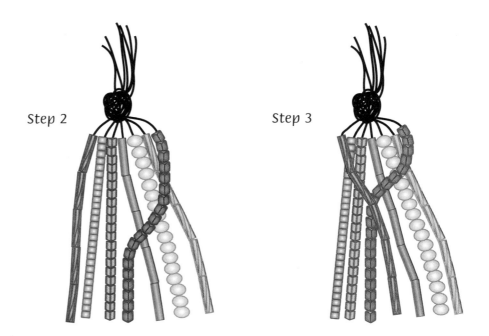

Step 2   Step 3

3 Next, bring the left-most strand over three strands and lay it down.

4 If you feel comfortable, you may hold all the strands in your hands while braiding. Keep the tension fairly tight. * Repeat between asterisks until you come to the end of the beads. The braid should measure 6". This measurement will vary depending on how tightly or loosely you braid. You might have to braid it over again if it is way too long or too short. Remove the stop beads making sure you hold the braid tight so it won't unravel. At this time also remove any excess beads, as the braiding process will make some of the strands longer than the others. Tie the strands into an overhand knot the same way you did at the other end of the braid. Make sure the knot is right up against the beads to hold the braid securely.

5 Thread all seven strands through a gold cone and pull the strands tightly so that the knot and the end of the braid are hidden in the cone. Then thread all seven strands through a clamshell bead tip. Tie a square knot using three strands of the thread for one side and four strands for the other, making sure the knot is all the way inside the clamshell. Clip any excess thread and place a drop of bonding glue onto the knot. Using flat-nosed pliers squeeze the clamshell shut over the knot. (If you prefer, you may attach the cones using eye pins, which are described on page 7.) With round-nose pliers, round off the hook at the end of the clamshell. Attach one end of the clasp with a jump ring. Repeat for the other side of the bracelet.

Continues

✳ Barrette

Materials
Nymo beading thread, black, size B
Beading needle, size 12
Gold-lined seed beads, size 11°
Pink-white heart seed bead, size 8°
Blue iris twist bugle beads, ¼" long
Gold AB luster bugle beads, ¼" long
Pink matte twist bugle beads, ¼" long
Bronze triangle beads
Matte iris AB triangle beads
1 gold barrette back
Bonding glue

1 Repeat Step 1 of the bracelet instructions, except make the strands 4" long.

2 Repeat Step 2 of the bracelet instructions.

3 Cover the barrette back with glue. Tuck the end knots under the braid so they are not visible and lay the braid evenly onto the barrette back. Press and hold for a minute; let sit until dry.

thread conditioners

The traditional thread conditioner is beeswax. Slide the thread through the wax several times to apply an even, light coating. Then, slide the thread between your fingers several times to soften the wax and press it into the thread. If you use too much wax, the eye of the needle can close from wax build-up and even the bead holes can get filled with wax. To remove a wax plug from a needle, hold the needle between your thumb and forefinger to warm the wax in the eye. Also, it is better to use a thicker thread instead of heavily waxing a thinner one to give body to the bead fabric.

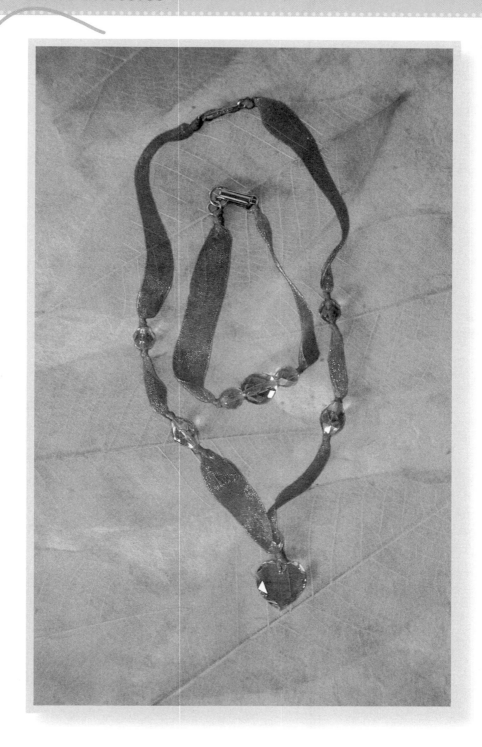

*W*ant to create that perfect token of affection for that person that makes your heart race? Then this crystal heart choker and matching bracelet are exactly what you need to chase the lovesick blues away.

Continues →

Choker

Materials
1 yard light blue gossamer ribbon, ½" wide
Twisted beading needle
1 crystal heart pendant bead
2 oval faceted crystal beads, 12mm x 9mm
2 round faceted crystal beads, 8mm
1 gold triangle to fit the heart bead
1 gold torpedo clasp
Embroidery scissors
Chain-nose pliers

1 When using ribbon, cut the end to facilitate bead stringing.

2 Thread the needle with the thin end. String on one side of the clasp and pull it beyond the cut part of the ribbon all the way down the ribbon to the other end, and tie an overhand knot. Bring the knot up close to the clasp before tightening. Trim off the short end of the ribbon to the knot.

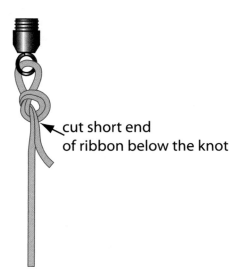

cut short end
of ribbon below the knot

3 Open the triangle and fit the open end into the hole in the heart. Carefully squeeze the triangle shut with the pliers.

4 String on one round bead (8mm), one oval bead (12mm x 9mm), the crystal heart, one oval bead (12mm x 9mm), and one round bead (8mm). Make an overhand knot 3" from the clasp. Slide the 8mm bead up to the knot and make another overhand knot, bringing the knot as close to the bead as possible. (See Techniques, page 16, for knot tying instructions.) Make another knot 1" away from the last knot. Slide the oval bead up to the knot and make another knot close to the bead. Slide the heart 2¼" away from the knot. Make an overhand knot using both sides of the ribbon, as in Step 2, only do not cut off the ribbon and have the triangle and the heart caught in the loop made by the knot. This will make the heart dangle. Make a knot 2" away from the heart knot. Knot and space the last two beads and clasp to match the first side of the choker.

Use smaller ribbon and smaller beads for a different look.

✳ Bracelet

Materials
1 yard light blue gossamer ribbon, ½" wide
Twisted beading needle
1 round faceted crystal bead, 12mm
2 round faceted crystal beads, 8mm
1 gold fold-over clasp
Embroidery scissors

1 Repeat Step 1 from the choker instructions.

2 String on one of each of the following: an 8mm bead, a 12mm bead, and another 8mm bead. Tie an overhand knot 2¾" away from clasp knot. Slide all three beads up against the knot and then tie another overhand knot as close to the beads as possible.

3 String on the other side of the clasp and tie it 2¾" away from the last bead knot. Cut off the excess ribbon.

If you're looking for something to wear on that special occasion, when you want to be fancy and simple at the same time, you've found it here. Accented with gold and bronze, this subtle set can either complement a black dress or offset a more lively color.

✳ Necklace

Materials
Nymo beading thread, black, size F
2 beading needles, size 12
91 purple luster hex beads, size 8°
193 silver-lined gold-cut Japanese tubular beads
91 iridescent dark purple seed beads, size 11°
50 black hex bugle beads, 5mm
3 iridescent black faceted teardrop beads, 8mm
1 bronze heart
2 gold bead tips
1 gold barrel clasp

1 Thread needles on each end of a 6-foot length of beading thread. Using one needle, string on one gold, one purple hex, one gold, one dark purple size 11°, one black bugle bead, one dark purple size 11°, one gold, one purple hex, one gold. Move these beads to the middle of the thread. String on one dark purple size 11°, one black bugle, one dark purple size 11°. Then pass the other needle through the beads in the opposite direction. * Using one of the needles, string on one gold, one purple hex, one gold. Now use the other needle to string on one gold, one purple hex, one gold. Push these beads down against the other beads. String on one dark purple size 11°, one black bugle bead, one dark purple size 11°. Then pass the other needle through the beads in the opposite direction. * Repeat between the asterisks 16 times or until the piece measures 3½".

bugle beads

Bugle beads are tube-shaped beads from 2mm to 30mm in length. These can be straight, hex cut, or twisted along their length.

2 With one of the needles, string on two gold beads, 1 faceted teardrop, then one dark purple size 11°, PNBT teardrop bead and string on two gold beads. On the other needle, string on two gold beads. Now string on one dark purple size 11°, one black bugle, one dark purple size 11°. Then pass the other needle through the beads in the opposite direction. Repeat between asterisks from Step 1, three times.

Continues

3 Using the same size needle as the first dangle from Step 2, string on two gold beads, one bugle, one purple hex, one bronze heart, one gold bead, one teardrop, one dark purple size 11°. PNBT teardrop, gold bead, heart, purple hex, black bugle, then string on two gold beads. Using the other needle, string on two gold beads. Now string on one dark purple size 11°, one black bugle, one dark purple size 11°. Then pass the other needle through the beads in the opposite direction. Repeat between asterisks from Step 1 three times.

4 Using the same size needle as from Steps 2 and 3, create the third dangle by repeating Step 2.

5 String on one dark purple size 11°, one black bugle, one dark purple size 11°. Repeat Step 1, between the asterisks, 16 times or until the piece measures 3½".

6 String on one gold, one bugle, one dark purple size 11°, one bugle, one gold. Do this on both needles separately. * Now thread both needles through one purple hex bead, one gold bead. * Repeat between asterisks for 1", adjusting length if necessary to fit your neck. Remember to make only half of the adjustment now and the other half on the other end of the necklace.

7 Attach the bead tip as close to the beads as possible and attach clasp to the bead tip.

beginning and ending threads

No matter how long a thread you use, eventually you have to end and restart your thread. For the best results, be sure to hide the threads invisibly in the work, secure them in the work with a small knot or by weaving around in a circle so the thread cannot come out, and bury the new end in the beads so it does not show.

8 Thread about 3 feet of thread with two needles. Pass one needle through the dark purple size 11°, black bugle and dark purple size 11° at the beginning of the necklace. Center the beads in the middle of the thread and repeat Step 6. Attaching the other end of the clasp by repeating Step 7.

✳ Earrings

Materials

2 purple luster hex beads, size 8°
4 silver-lined gold-cut Japanese tubular beads
2 black hex bugle beads, 5mm
2 black iridescent faceted teardrop beads, 8mm
2 iridescent dark purple seed beads, size 11°
2 bronze heart beads
2 gold head pins
2 gold kidney ear wires
Flat-nose pliers
Round-nose pliers

Continues

1 Put one dark purple size 11° seed bead, one teardrop, one gold, one heart, one purple hex, one bugle, and one gold bead onto a head pin.

2 Bend the end of the wire at a 90° angle close to the last bead with the flat-nose pliers.

3 Using needle-nose pliers hold the wire just above the bend and wrap the wire around pliers making a small loop (Step 3). Before closing the loop, slip on the earring wire. Cut wire with wire cutters and close the loop with the flat-nose pliers.

4 Repeat Steps 1, 2, and 3 for other earring.

pliers

A pair of needle-nose pliers is a necessity. If you live in an all-male household, purchase the daintiest, most delicate, pink-handled pliers available. Otherwise, pliers will "turn up" missing or greasy! As the budget allows, purchase round-nose pliers, crimping pliers and wire cutters, which are useful additions to a toolbox.

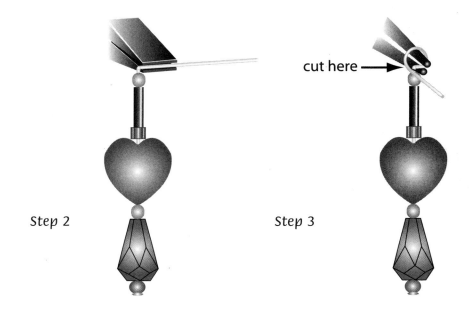

cut here

Step 2   *Step 3*

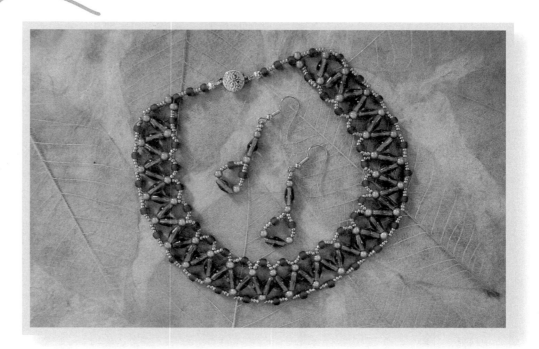

This intricate necklace is so colorful and vibrant that you'll think that you plucked it from the depths of the ocean's clear refreshing waters. Equally as refreshing will be the compliments you'll garner while wearing your creation.

 ## Necklace

Materials
Nymo beading thread, white or light blue, size F
2 beading needles, size 11
49 light green wonder beads, 4mm
294 metallic green seed beads, size 11°
53 matte cobalt blue seed beads, size 6°
44 blue transparent bi-cone beads, 10mm x 6mm
2 silver clamshell bead tips
1 silver round insert-style clasp
Round-nose pliers
Flat-nose pliers

Continues

1 Thread needle with 2 yards of thread. Leave a 12" tail. String on one wonder bead, one blue bi-cone, one wonder bead, one blue bi-cone, one wonder bead, three metallic beads, three cobalt beads, three metallic beads, and then PNBT the first wonder bead strung on, one blue bi-cone, and the next wonder bead. This is the first "stitch" (**Figure 1**). String three metallic beads, one cobalt, three metallics, three wonder beads, one blue bi-cone. Next PNT the third wonder bead strung on from the first "stitch." This makes the second "stitch" (**Figure 2**). String on three metallics, one cobalt, three metallics, one wonder bead, one blue bi-cone. PNT wonder bead strung on in the second stitch. This makes the third "stitch" (**Figure 3**). Repeat the third "stitch" 40 times, or until piece measures 10½", keeping thread tension tight throughout. Make sure you end with a chevron (both ends look alike with the "V" going up). Tie an overhand knot and weave thread end back through the beads until secure and cut off excess. Do the same thing to the thread tail at the beginning of the necklace.

Figure 1

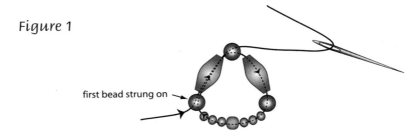

first bead strung on

Figure 2

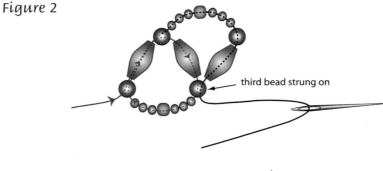

third bead strung on

Figure 3

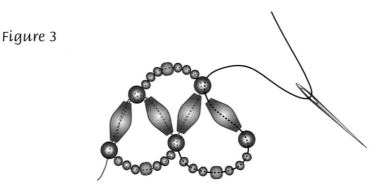

2 Thread the needle with about a two-foot length of thread, PNT one wonder bead, one blue bi-cone, and one wonder bead at one end of the necklace. Move the thread through the beads so that they are in the center of the thread (**Figure 4**). Thread another needle on the other end of the thread. String on three metallic, one cobalt, three metallic, and one wonder bead, to one of the thread ends and three metallic, one cobalt, three metallic, and one wonder bead to the other (**Figure 5**). Now using both needles at the same time so that both threads go through the beads, string on one cobalt, one metallic, one cobalt, three metallics, one cobalt (**Figure 6**). Attach a bead tip. Now attach one end of the clasp to the bead tip. Repeat on the other end of the necklace.

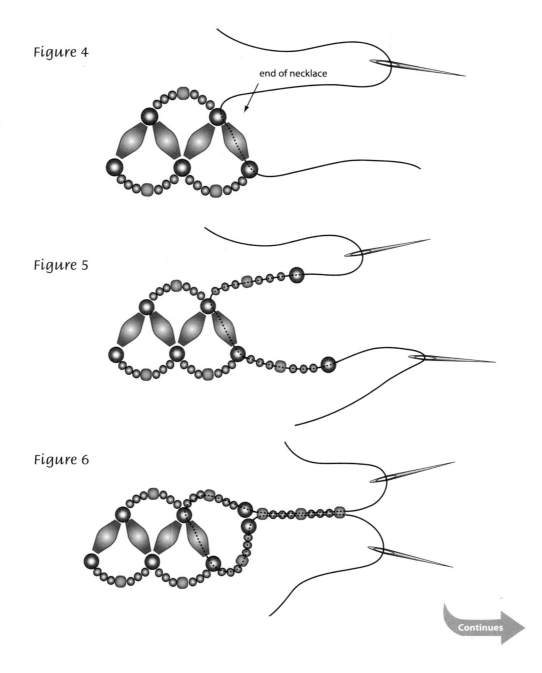

Figure 4

end of necklace

Figure 5

Figure 6

Continues

✳ *Earrings*

Materials

Nymo beading thread, white or light blue, size F
Beading needle, size 11
8 light green wonder beads, 4mm
36 metallic green seed beads, size 11°
4 matte cobalt blue seed beads, size 6°
4 blue transparent bi-cone beads, 10mm x 6mm
1 pair of silver fishhook ear wires
Round-nose pliers
Flat-nose pliers

1 Thread a needle with a length of thread about one yard long. String on six metallic beads, one wonder bead, one blue bi-cone, one wonder bead, three metallics, one cobalt, three metallics, one wonder bead, one blue bi-cone, one wonder bead, three metallics, one cobalt, and three metallics. Make sure the beads are in the middle of the thread. PNBT the second wonder bead strung on, the first blue bi-cone strung on, and the first wonder bead strung on.

square knot

When tying a square knot, always remember: right over left, then left over right. This means cross the thread in your right hand over the thread in your left hand and around and through to tie a knot. Then, cross the thread that's now in your left hand over the thread in your right hand and around and through to tie a knot again. This makes a secure knot that won't slip out as easily as others. You may also want to put a small amount of clear nail polish on the knot to make sure it stays tied.

2 PNT the loop on the bottom of the ear wire and PNBT the first six metallic beads strung on (**Figure 1**). PNBT beads until thread comes out where the thread went in and make a square knot using both thread ends (**Figure 2**). Hide the knot in a bead and pass the thread ends through several beads, then cut off the excess.

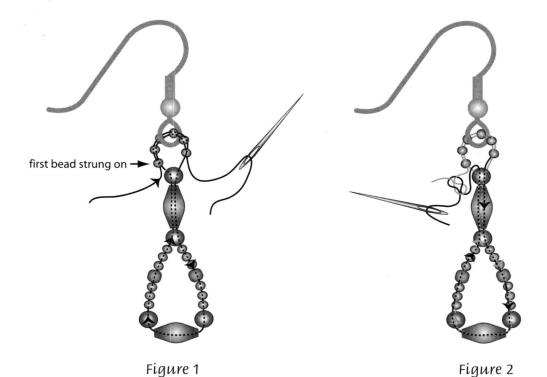

first bead strung on →

Figure 1   Figure 2

*T*he perfect pick-me-up for any gloomy day, this set is like carrying a bit of sunshine with you wherever you go. The bright topaz and the regal lavender work on almost any occasion.

✳ Necklace

Materials
Nymo beading thread, white, size F
Beading needle, size 11
56 topaz round faceted glass beads, 5mm
1 topaz round faceted glass bead, 7mm
10 gms gold luster amethyst Japanese tubular beads
2 gold bead tips
1 gold barrel clasp
Round-nose pliers
Flat-nose pliers

1 Using about 6 yards of thread, string 12 amethyst beads leaving an 8" tail. Make a circle by PNBT the first bead strung on (**Figure 1**). String on one topaz bead (5mm), PNT the sixth bead from the first bead strung on (**Figure 2**). * String on one amethyst, PNT adjacent bead on circle, string on one amethyst bead. PNT the first bead just strung on (**Figure 3**). String on 10 amethyst beads, PNT the second bead strung on from the two amethysts strung on just before these 10 (**Figure 4**). String on one topaz bead (5mm), PNT the sixth bead strung on.* Repeat between asterisks 25 times.

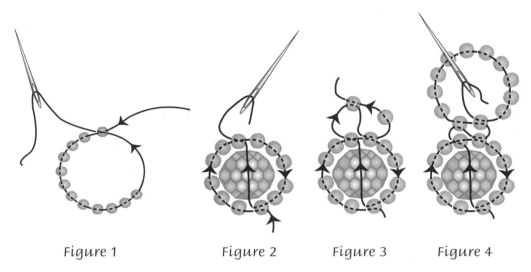

Figure 1   Figure 2   Figure 3   Figure 4

2 PNBT the next three beads of the circle so that the needle is coming out of the bottom of the daisy (**Figure 5**). Make three more daisies; then make a daisy using the 7mm topaz bead and 15 amethyst beads instead of 10. When you are done with the big daisy, PNBT the beads of the daisies of the dangle so that the thread is coming out on the opposite side of the top daisy (**Figure 6**).

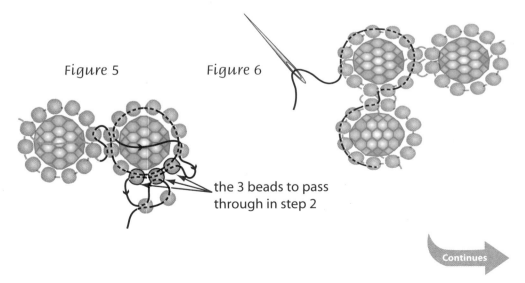

Figure 5   Figure 6

the 3 beads to pass
through in step 2

107

Continues ➡

3 Continue in the daisy chain making more daisies for the other side of the necklace.

4 Attach bead tips to each end of the necklace and then attach the clasp ends to the bead tips.

✳ Bracelet

Materials
Nymo beading thread, white, size F
Beading needle, size 11
23 topaz round faceted glass beads, 5mm
276 gold luster amethyst Japanese tubular beads
2 gold bead tips
1 gold barrel clasp
Round-nose pliers
Flat-nose pliers

1 Make the bracelet the same way as the necklace, but omitting the dangle. This bracelet has 23 daisies.

2 Attach the bead tips to the ends of the bracelet and then attach the clasp ends to the bead tips.

bead packaging

Beads can be packaged for sale in several ways. They are usually packaged by the bag or tube, by the hank or strand, or loose. Bags or tubes of beads are usually sold by weight, in grams and sometimes in ounces. A hank of beads is usually twelve 18- to 20-inch strands of beads with the ends tied together. Loose beads are usually large or specialty beads sold individually.

This beautiful necklace was designed by Amy Gourley. Inspired by jewelry worn in the Victorian era, these pieces speak to a more refined and demure form of beauty. Subtle grace and soothing colors add a distinctive flair to this project.

Continues ➔

Necklace

Materials

26-gauge gold wire, 5 feet
Figaro gold chain, 5 yards
1 gold fishhook clasp
2 fancy separator bars
15 gold jump rings
14 carnelian beads, 6mm

7 carnelian beads, 8mm
1 red glass drop bead, 1"
Side-style wire cutters
Chain-nose pliers
Round-nose pliers

1 First make the two small daisies. Use about 24" of the 26-gauge wire for each daisy. String six carnelian beads (6mm) onto the wire. Move the beads to the center of the wire. String the wire back through the first bead strung on forming a circle (**Figure 1**). String on one carnelian bead (6mm) and pass the wire through the fourth bead of the bead circle (this is a daisy chain stitch; see **Figure 2**). Make a wrapped loop (see Techniques, page 14, on how to make a wrapped loop) on each of the wire ends as close to the beads as possible (**Figure 3**). Make another one.

Figure 1   Figure 2   Figure 3

2 Now make the large daisy. Use about 36" of 26-gauge wire. Repeat the directions for the small daisies only use the 8mm carnelian beads. Make only one wrapped loop and on the other end of the wire just wrap it twice around the circle wire between the two beads. Use a jump ring to attach the drop bead to the wrapped loop. Now attach two jump rings between beads two and three and between beads four and five (**Figure 4**).

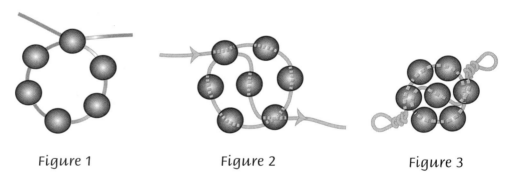

jump ring   jump ring

jump ring

Figure 4

3 Cut four lengths of chain 3¼" long, four lengths of chain 3½" long and four lengths of chain 4" long. Attach the chains with the short ones on top, medium ones in the middle, and the long ones on the bottom. Use jump rings to attach the chain to all four of the wrapped loops on the small daisies and use the two jump rings already attached to the large daisy to attach the chains to the large daisy (**Figure 5**). Attach the end lengths of chain to the separator bars with jump rings (**Figure 6**). Make sure you keep the chains in the right order so they don't twist.

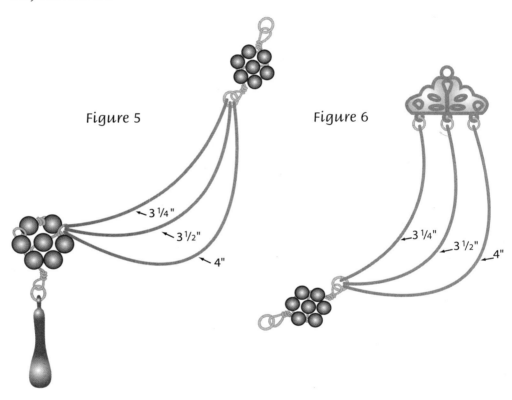

Figure 5   Figure 6

4 Use jump rings to attach the clasp to the separator bars.

✳ Earrings

Materials
26-gauge gold wire, 14"
2 gold jump rings
2 red glass drop beads, 1"

2 carnelian beads, 8mm
2 gold fishhook ear wires

Continues

1 Cut a 7" length of 26-gauge wire. String on one carnelian bead (8mm) and move the bead to the middle of the wire. Make a wrapped wire loop on each end as close to the bead as possible. Attach a red drop bead to one of the wrapped wire loops using a jump ring.

2 Using needle-nose pliers, open the loop on the end of the ear wire. Slip the wrapped loop that doesn't have the drop bead on it into the loop of the earring wire and close the loop with the needle-nose pliers. Repeat Steps 1 and 2 for the other earring.

faceted beads

Faceted beads are seed beads that have been ground with one or more flat surfaces. These include charlottes, three-cuts, and Austrian Swarovski crystals.

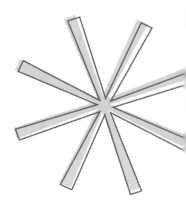

Resources

Here is a listing of books and Web sites that can be helpful to you in your quest for more beading instruction and beading supplies.

Books

Step-by-Step Bead Stringing by Ruth F. Poris (Golden Hands Press, 2001)
This title explores the very basic technique of stringing beads to create gorgeous jewelry.

Out on a Loom by Margie Deeb (Minoa, 1999)
This book shares fun ways to use a loom while beading.

The Complete Guide to Beading Techniques by Jane Davis (Krause, 2001)
This title serves as the ultimate guide to techniques and gives you the knowledge necessary in which to master them.

Beading Basics by Mary Sotri (C&T Publishing, 2004)
This book is a colorful, helpful guide to walk you through beginner beading concepts.

Complete Beading for Beginners by Karen Rempel (Harbour Publishing, 1996)
This is another title that offers tips, advice, and instructions for mastering the beading craft.

Web Sites

www.beadwork.about.com
This site shows you how to bead jewelry and other projects and is a valuable tool to find out more information about beading techniques and patterns.

www.firemountaingems.com

This site is a supplier of gems and beads and also supplies clasps, mountings, and settings, as well as helpful resources for continued beading success.

www.wire-sculpture.com

This site has a huge selection of beads to choose from and offers discount tools and materials, instructional DVDs and videos, as well as free patterns and a craft newsletter you can subscribe to.

www.allcrafts.net

This site shows you the ins and outs of jewelry making with beads in addition to a variety of other crafts, including wedding, kids, and nature crafts.

www.beadandbutton.com

This site is home to the magazine ***Bead & Button***, which offers a wealth of information involving the beading craft.

practice!

Beginners often seem disappointed with the caliber of their beadwork. Every other skill requires hours, even years of practice to achieve competency. Why shouldn't beadwork? It may be necessary to make several versions of the same project before the bead artist feels it is "perfect." Actually, Native Americans have the right idea with their spirit bead concept. The spirit bead is an intentional mistake in the beadwork to remind humankind that mere humans cannot expect to achieve perfection. So, don't focus on the mistakes; look at the skills attained and practice, practice, practice.

Acknowledgments

A very special thanks to **Elizabeth Gourley** and **Ellen Talbott,** who contributed projects for this publication:

Index

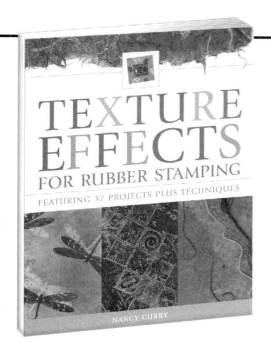

the best in
rubber stamping techniques
from *North Light Books!*

It's easy to add rich beauty to personalized cards and gifts!

Add elegant, rich textures to your handmade greeting cards and gifts. With complete, step-by-step instructions and 37 stylish projects, you'll find a wonderful mix of new texture approaches, dimensional effects and decorative accents to make your personalized cards and gifts more memorable.

#33014-K • $22.99

Be sure to look for these rubber stamping titles:

Creative Stamping with Mixed Media Techniques
#32315-K • $22.99

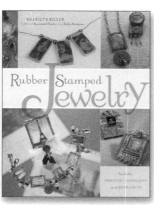

Rubber Stamped Jewelry
#32415-K • $22.99

Stamp Your Stuff!
#32432-K • $12.99

30-Minute Rubber Stamp Workshop
#32142-K • $24.99

The trusted source for rubber stampers

Savings Code
TL04ERSB

the best in
polymer clay techniques
from *North Light Books!*

Create Unique, Sophisticated Gifts!

Use the beauty and versatility of polymer clay to create elegant gifts your family and friends will adore. Lisa Pavelka guides you in creating 20 polymer clay projects using the latest techniques for a variety of stunning gift ideas in *Elegant Gifts in Polymer Clay.*

Through detailed direction you'll discover easy-to-follow methods for creating tortoise shell effects, rich enameled surfaces, the marbled look of mokumé gané, foil resists and faux mother-of-pearl. You'll use these techniques to create gifts such as a toasting goblet, a key rack, a votive candleholder and more!

#33028 • $22.99

Be sure to look for these polymer clay titles:

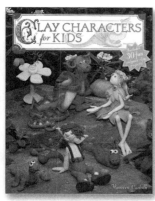  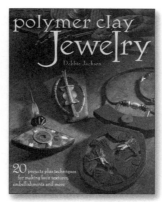 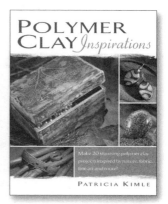

Clay Characters for Kids
#32161-K • $12.99

Fast Polymer Clay
#32703-K • $19.99

Polymer Clay Jewelry
#32873-K • $22.99

Polymer Clay Inspirations
#33013-K • $22.99

The trusted source for creative crafters

the best in

wedding crafts & inspirations

from **North Light Books, Memory Makers Books** and **Betterway Books!**

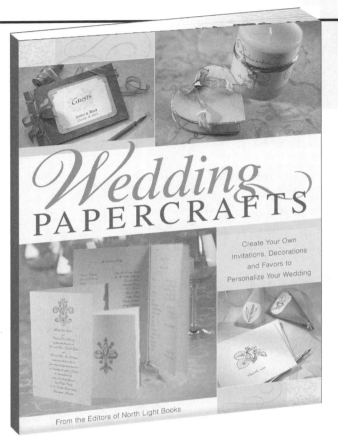

Wedding PAPERCRAFTS

Create Your Own Invitations, Decorations and Favors to Personalize Your Wedding

From the Editors of North Light Books

Make your wedding a unique and memorable event!

You'll discover over 50 personalized projects to make your wedding one-of-a-kind. Easy-to-follow instructions guide you in creating professional-looking invitations and coordinated projects such as guest books, party favors, decorations, keepsakes and more. From whimsical and contemporary to elegant and sophisticated, you're sure to find inspiration to reflect your personal style for a wedding that is truly your own.

#70603-K • $19.99

Be sure to look for these wedding craft titles:

Intimate Weddings
#70642-K • $14.99

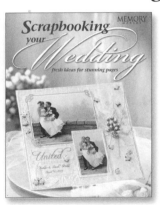

Scrapbooking Your Wedding
#33211-K • $22.99

New Inspirations in Wedding Florals
#70582-K • $19.99

How to Have a Big Wedding on a Small Budget
#70594-K • $14.99

The trusted source for brides-to-be

Available at craft stores, fine booksellers everywhere, or toll free at 1-800-448-0915.

North Light Books, Memory Makers Books, and Betterway Books are members of the F+W Publications, Inc. family.

NORTH LIGHT BOOKS BETTER WAY BOOKS MEMORY MAKERS BOOKS